AUTUMN IN BROOKLYN

September-November 1978

AUTUMN IN BROOKLYN

September-November 1978

RICHARD GRAYSON

Superstition Mountain Press

Phoenix – 2009

Printed in the United States of America.

Superstition Mountain Press
4303 Cactus Road
Phoenix, AZ 85032

First Edition

ISBN 978-0-578-03208-5

10 9 8 7 6 5 4 3 2 1

For Louis Strick

Autumn in Brooklyn:
September – November 1978

Monday, September 4, 1978

8 PM. I feel rather sad about the summer ending. It seems impossible that three months has passed since my birthday. I've always thought of the new year as beginning now rather than in January, and I still feel that way (even though this year's Rosh Hashona is a month away). It's chilly out now and today was sunny but just a bit too cool for swimming.

I spent the afternoon with Josh – we drove around, played pinball at Buddy's, chatted in the backyard. He's just as sour on life as he always was; maybe he's even worse. He and Simon went to the Eighth Street Bookshop to get an *ABC to Literary Magazines* by R.C. Morse, which I told him about. He said he saw Alice there, rummaging through magazines looking for a story by me. Laura mentioned staying with Peter Spielberg on the Cape, and Josh and Simon made the mistake of putting Peter down in front of her; she cooled considerably after hearing their comments.

Josh and his friend Fat Ronnie want to start a literary magazine called *Moron*; the name expresses their general philosophy. Josh's unemployment, now $125, has only 6 more weeks to run, and he'd rather do anything than go back to driving an oil truck this winter. Josh would like to get into advertising, but even when he offers his services for free, he's turned down. And the fact that he's had no sex for six months is depressing him. All the old Jewish people in his building bug him; they think he and Simon are lovers.

Simon is very confused about his future and may stay another month at Josh's before he figures out his next move – probably back to Manhattan. Josh is very broke and needs to come up with something soon. He's still got his "life sucks" attitude and that can't help.

I won't say that the condition of Josh, Simon, Ralph, Michael Kramer, etc., pleases me, but at least in some ways I am more 'together' than any of them. I'm terrified about going to Albany and it's going to take much of the next few months to adjust to the idea of going there, but I really do think it will be a good move for me. True, I'm making it in desperation because I cannot keep living at home and teaching part-time at LIU, but it looks as though nothing's going to "rescue" me from moving.

I don't think I'm going to be writing all that much this fall, but once I get to Albany, I think I'll have time, distance and even loneliness working for me. Nothing spectacular is going to happen between now and January. I'll be very concerned about Dad's surgery and Grandma Ethel's condition too, but there's not much I can do about those thing. I expect Ronna and I will still be seeing each other, though less often; I guess we both want it that way. And deep down I don't really think much will come of meeting Bill-Dale although I hope that something – just a good friendship, maybe – does.

There's a briskness in the air that seems to say "get on with it"; there's not much else I can do anyway. Tomorrow I'll get a haircut and hand in my grades in the Novel course at LIU and for the next couple of weeks I don't really know what I'll be doing. I do think that right now *living* is more important to me than writing and that my major efforts will be here in this diary.

I don't expect any 'big' acceptances or stories coming out and in a way I need that less and less. Maybe this loss of desperation will be good for me. School is in the air, and one part of me wishes I was beginning my graduate work in Albany now instead of in January.

This morning I worked on a letter and a letter of credit and bill of lading for Dad, who's ordering 3000 pairs of new jeans; I just hope they get here from Hong Kong in time for Christmas. Marc's car hasn't been found yet, and I'm beginning to doubt that it ever will be.

Tuesday, September 6, 1978

9 PM. Years ago, when I was an undergraduate, my diary was mostly a collection of the doings of other people. Once I was so involved with my Brooklyn College friends, but now there are only a handful who mean anything to me. A few weeks ago Ronna told me that Ivan had gotten married, but I hadn't thought that was important enough to record until now.

Yesterday Josh spotted Stacy walking out of a restaurant with some guy and I didn't even look up to catch a glimpse of her. Today Elihu told me that Leon has moved to San Francisco and that Jerry has moved back to New York City, but these things don't really matter to me anymore. I used to be obsessed with Ivan, Stacy, Jerry and Leon, but now I'm only mildly interested in their lives. I feel just about as interested as someone I know only vaguely, like Les Kravitz, who's running for the Assembly in this district.

But I can see I'm protesting too much, and besides, I do like to tie up loose ends (that's the novelist in me). So let's gossip: Mikey told me that Mike is leaving Fordham for the CUNY Graduate Center because of personality conflicts and that Bob Lefkowitz owns a P.R. firm in New Jersey. Elihu mentioned that Richard Pontone is also running for the state legislature; it's amazing how many BC people are running for office. Rhoda Jacobs, whom Elihu is working for, will probably make it to the Assembly this year.

Elihu said he was in a bar (gay, of course) when someone he vaguely recognized came over to him: it was Jerry. He left Madison because he needed a change; he left with some money and hopes to get some kind of no-show job, the kind he's always had starting with his job for Mayor Lindsay. Jerry's living just down the block from Elihu on Henry Street. He said that Leon was unhappy in Wisconsin and left flat broke for San Francisco, where he seems unable to get a job. And Shelli's doing just fine with her TV work; she plans to stay in Madison indefinitely. So that's the story with people from my past. I *am* curious about them, after all – but I do not want them to be a part of my future.

This morning I went to LIU to hand in my grades. Terry Malley said he saw the article on me on Page Six in the *Post*. Margaret told me she'd let me know about courses by the end of next week. This afternoon I got a call from a Prof. Oscar Miller at Kingsborough; the chairman had given him my resumé (I'm sure he wouldn't have if had I not used Annette Fisher's name). I have an interview with Miller tomorrow although there are probably no courses available to teach. If there are, and if they let me teach them, I'll be very pleasantly surprised. I'm a fatalist now, remember?

I got a much-needed haircut this afternoon (the sun has bleached my hair so nicely that the woman who shampooed it asked, "Is that your natural color? Oh, you're so lucky!") and then exercised, lay in the sun and swam (I've begun to enjoy being in the pool so much these last few days). I got a nice postcard from Ian Young up in Toronto – St. Martin's is still considering the gay story anthology. This evening I called Michael Kramer, who's been ill with a colitis-like ailment (he's going to a specialist next week although it may just be nerves) and I also spoke to Carolyn Bennett, who's busy trying to meet her weekly deadlines at Courier-Life.

<u>Wednesday, September 6, 1978</u>

5 PM. At the moment I'm annoyed with Dad for trying to make me feel guilty about not working for him tomorrow when the jeans come in. But I'm staying out late tonight and I had planned to for a week or more, and I don't intend to get up early and break my back tomorrow. I'm under no obligation to Dad. I may have to start work as early as next Tuesday and I don't want to give up my vacation. If he wants a helper, why can't he ask Jonny? As you can tell, I *am* feeling guilty but I refuse to let that guilt overwhelm me.

I had an interview at Kingsborough today – it certainly is a beautiful school: the architecture of the campus is striking and it's nice being on the ocean. Prof. Miller, the director of freshman English, questioned me about my background, philosophy of teaching and my LIU experience; I disagreed with him about several things but the only "right" answers I was interested in giving were the ones I felt.

Their remedial courses are being restructured this term and their new English 01 course is probably beyond me, as I've never taught reading. I can teach their English 11, a 4-hour course equivalent to English 10 at LIU – a remedial writing class -- and I could also teach their standard freshman composition course, which they number 12.

If any course are available, Miller said, he'd call me between tomorrow and Monday. Classes start on Tuesday. The only problem is that their classes meet 4 times a week and that might interfere with my courses at LIU. Of course Kingsborough is a CUNY school and they pay much better than LIU does; if I got 2 courses there, I might not want to take 2 courses at LIU, as it would leave me with little time to write (or live).

The best thing to do for now is to play it by ear and see what develops. Kingsborough might not even call me, and in a way I am a bit frightened about being in a new teaching environment. LIU is so warm and comfortable and familiar to me by now that there's no tension in it. But if I am to go to Albany in the spring, I'd better get used to new places; besides, community college experience couldn't hurt.

I had trouble getting to sleep last night; I thought I felt very fatalistic, but really I don't, and I'm still not sure I'm capable of going through life with a passive attitude. And I'm not certain I want to.

I got another letter from Bill-Dale today; he's not bothered by my being 27, but says he can't come in to New York and asks if I can visit him at Rutgers, especially on weekends when his roommate is away. I suppose I could manage to get my battered Comet down to New Brunswick and back, but already I'm beginning to have pinpricks of doubts about Bill-Dale.

He sent me an article he'd written, an attack on the plastic America of the 1970s; he writes well, but he's concerned with things that I stopped being concerned with years ago. I haven't been an idealist for a long time now, and I lived through the years 1968-1972 and don't think of them as the kind of idyllic period Bill-Dale assumes they were.

It's probably a function of our ages. I was in college during the turmoil years, the protest/hippie years, and I went through rallies, demonstrations, office takeovers. Bill-Dale arrived at Rutgers in 1974 in the midst of the post-Watergate recession, when all the students went back into conservatism, fraternities and making money, so he missed the days of what we might call the counterculture.

Bill-Dale is almost rigid in his idealism while I am a pragmatist, willing to settle for half a loaf of whole wheat bread, and I am not offended by shopping malls, McDonald's and discos – or people who smoke pot. So I'm not sure we're on the same wavelength, but I would still like to meet him.

Thursday, September 7, 1978

5 PM. Last night I had one of the worst cases of insomnia I've ever had. I lay in bed sleepless until well after 6 AM, when I had a dream of rage against my mother. Then I awoke at 9 AM, when Pearl Hochstadt called, inviting me to a preview of a paper on grading she'll be giving. Today was one of those surreal days.

Why couldn't I sleep? My mind was whirring with so many different thoughts: Ronna and how we haven't been as close as I'd hoped; Bill-Dale and his dogmatic idealism and what might come of that; despite myself, guilt over not working for Dad, worry over Dad's surgery and Grandma Ethel's illness; the un-September-like hot weather; the details of the House Assassination Committee testimony, on TV all day – Mrs. Connally saying she heard Jackie moan,

"They've killed my husband. . . I'm holding his brain in my hand"; of the possibility of teaching at Kingsborough and the fear that that arises within me; the wonder at how I can possibly move to Albany if I can't cope with little changes; Andreas telling Alice and April that I've gone the farthest of any of them in my career; my inability or unwillingness to write any fiction in the past three weeks; the outbreak of Legionnaire's disease in the Garment Center; Jerry being back in town; money worries; a story beginning with the sentence, "Only failures need to succeed"; and so much more.

I feel very unsettled; I am having difficulty adjusting to the changes and the forthcoming changes in my life. Formerly I had always tried to make sense of my confusion through my writing, but I don't seem able to do that any longer. I haven't written a first-rate story since late July, when they took my rented IBM typewriter away.

Am I doing the right thing in going to Albany? What if I hate it up there? What if everyone hates me? What if I can't write up there? What if I can't survive on my own? Dr. Lippmann invited me to visit him, but I don't want to appear as confused as I was when I was his patient a decade ago. I don't know what it is I do need – probably just time – and it's hard for me to learn patience.

I met Alice last night and we had dinner at
Shakespeare's and brought each other up on current
goings-on. Alice and Philip have been fighting, but
she proposed to him, asking him to marry her in
February 1980, but Philip said no, he doesn't want to
marry here and he wanted to live with her only for
financial reasons.

Philip's comedy, *Hotel Marilyn*, is going into rehearsal
soon; if it makes off-Broadway, Philip might be able
to get out of his financial bind, which was
compounded when his apartment was robbed
recently. Alice feels that her career is at a standstill;
although she met her goal of making $3,000
freelancing this year, she's beginning to feel, as April
says, that they're doing "hack work." Andreas
lectured them and told them to emulate me and do
more "important" writing. I don't think either of
them can afford it.

After dinner Alice and I walked among what she
called the "hoi polloi" along Fifth Avenue – she
confuses the word with its opposite. (I have similar
problems with "nonplussed" and "enervated.") We
played Scrabble and a word game and of course Alice
won. She asked me if she's changed since moving to
Manhattan. I said no. Alice told of meeting Hal for
lunch (that fool still hasn't finished his dissertation)
and of her desire to stir up trouble and call Scott
again. She also embarrassed me by reading *Disjointed
Fictions* aloud.

Friday, September 8, 1978

5 PM. Again I had terrible insomnia last night, not
getting to sleep until 5:30 AM. With three of these
difficult nights in a row, there's no question that I'm
in a state of turmoil. It all concerns moving to
Albany, of course. I torture myself with the question:
Am I doing the right thing? I am quite terrified of
being 300 miles away from all my friends, family and
familiar surroundings. My doubts come in two
varieties: psychological and practical.

Practically speaking, I don't know if a Doctor of Arts
degree will do me any good at this point in my career.
Is it worth spending the money? Psychologically, of
course, I have doubts about my ability to function
away from everyone and everything I've known. I
fear a breakdown, a total inability to function, and I
wonder if I'm wise to just throw myself into a phobic
situation without leading up to it – by getting an
apartment in the city, for example. Secretly I've been
hoping that something would happen – a miracle – to
"save" me from going to Albany.

Last night I got the idea that maybe I should apply to
Rutgers, which is much closer, and where I might feel
more comfortable. But then again, I'm not sure I want
to go to graduate school at all. Oh, I'm so confused

it's no wonder I can't sleep. I feel myself becoming ill and I'm almost certain to come down with a cold.

Outside it's turned rainy and very cool – it may go down to 50° tonight. See, I don't want to be thought of as a coward – which is pretty much what Mom assumed when I attempted to speak to her this morning. I've told all my friends I'm going to Albany, and I suppose I don't want to look foolish – although I'm sure most of them couldn't care less, or, like Alice (who said to me, "Albany is not the only way to leave home"), actively discourage me from going up there.

I just don't know what to do. It's only 4 months away. I know I have to trust my feelings, but at this point I can't sort out my feelings to the stage where I know what's what. There's nobody to talk to, either – I wish I had a counselor or therapist.

Nobody called from Kingsborough so I guess that's out – and in a way, teaching there would have provided me with the extra income to increase my options. I feel a bit suicidal, a I can see no happy solution – but on the hand, this is going to be a growing-up transition as painful as earlier ones. I haven't felt this lost since Shelli left me seven years ago; I went through a terrible time then and I expect another terrible time coming up. Is this pain necessary and useful or is there an easier way to gain independence?

Last night Alison called and asked if I could help her look for an apartment while Ronna's away in Pennsylvania. Now, Alison has left her own past to start a new life in a strange city, so why can't I? Am I, unlike Ronna or Alison or Avis or others, some kind of delicate emotional cripple?

If tonight is another sleepless night, I think I will go insane. And this is supposed to be my "vacation"! I did write a little last evening, but I feel too pressured to be creative. I wish I could work this all out by myself, but maybe I need professional help.

Meanwhile, I feel exhausted and lost and feverish. I see myself getting ill because of lack of sleep and because it would almost be a relief. I'm going to try to get out of the house now, though, and see if I can lift my spirits. This is the third dark and depressing Friday in a row. I feel too depressed to deal with any of my responsibilities and obligations.

Saturday, September 9, 1978

11 PM. I feel considerably more cheerful now than I have been feeling. Yesterday, after writing my diary entry, I went out to dinner and a movie, the very good *Buddy Holly Story*. I identified with Buddy, who was an innovative artist going his own way. And I slept well last night, breaking the insomnia cycle at

last – so even if I don't fall asleep right away tonight, I won't feel so desperate.

See, I think I really *do* want to move to Albany. Today, when I read about the program in the AWP Newsletter, it excited me. It's just that I'm terribly frightened. But I want to face that fear and move past it – think how proud and happy I'll be *then*.

This morning the perfect-bound copies of *Disjointed Fictions* arrived, and they look so much nicer than the saddle-stitched ones. Despite the flaws in the book's type, layout and design, I'm proud of the material inside.

Today's mail also brought a book by Richard Kostelanetz on the politics of grants – he's an egomaniac but a very engaging writer, and most of the time he's right. The dilemma for a young writer like myself seems to be walking a narrow tightrope, trying to please the establishment (CAPS and NEA grant committees) while maintaining artistic integrity. It ain't easy.

I long for respectability. My book's bio notes include my "establishment" credits: Bread Loaf Scholar, LIU teacher, Fiction Collective, *Texas Quarterly*, *Shenandoah, Epoch*. And the material in *Disjointed Fictions* isn't likely to please the powers that be.

But what do I care, right? I haven't been writing
lately and I don't even care that much. I refuse to
keep repeating my earlier successes and must move
on to newer subjects and forms. Sending out ten
submissions today made me realize the paucity of
first-rate material I have on hand.

And yes, really, I'd rather not write than turn out
second-rate stuff. I told Louis Strick that I'm still an
apprentice, and I have to believe that; I have
confidence in my work, but I have a long way to go.

I visited my grandparents today; also visiting them
was their remarkable neighbor Jean Grey, who read
my book and said, "You are as crazy as a bedbug, but
you're intelligent, I can see that." Jean is 80, the
widow of a dentist. She drives her own car, reads
voraciously, goes to museums and keeps up with
current events.

We had an interesting conversation; most people
would probably think old people have nothing to say,
but they're wrong. A woman like Jean is as young in
her mind as many 25-year-olds. She gave me a good
line about nepotism: "His father took a liking to him
and made him a partner."

And she told about this young girl who loves to do
somersaults. I saw her on my way out: a scraggly-
blond barefoot brat, she did a somersault on request
for me. Jean had asked her how she, Jean, could learn

to do somersaults and the girl said, "It's easy. Just get young."

Grandma wondered why she hadn't seen me lately; I felt bad that I've neglected her, especially now. The lotion is clearing up some of her red, but it's also spreading to new places. I don't think Grandma Ethel has any idea of how serious a condition her lymphoma is – or maybe she refuses to acknowledge it.

We had coffee and talked. Grandpa Herb repeated the same old stories I've heard a zillion times before – like him having to walk me on the boardwalk at 5 AM because my crying annoyed everyone in the bungalow court. His brother Jack is in the hospital and seems to be dying: "He looks like Abe did at the end."

Sunday, September 10, 1978

I just got off the phone with Mason, who's back in Rockaway after landing a teaching job at the junior high school near Grandma Ethel's house – the same junior high he and Mikey and everyone in Belle Harbor went to. It's nice that Mason finally has, as he called it, "a real job," and he'll be doing well financially now. And maybe we can see more of each other. (I did not mention my moving to Albany.)

We gossiped a lot. Mason doesn't know that Libby's sleeping with Grant and he was jealous that Brian McIntosh wrote, after visiting Portland, that he'd "like to take Libby back to South Dakota with me." Mikey thinks Mason should be over Libby by now, and perhaps he's right, but I'm not going to be the one to tell him that she's living with a guy.

David White and Angie visited Mason upstate and he was surprised when they slept in the same bed. But David told him that he just happened to be around when Angie and Libby's brother Chuck broke up and that their relationship is mostly a friendship: he knows Angie's got to grow. Mason speculated that Angie brings out the paternal instinct in all of us; I know I feel that way about her.

Mason mentioned running into Stacy, who finally went to her dreamland, California – and, as expected, she returned terribly disappointed. Stacy had always set up unreasonable expectations of some kind of paradise out there. Mason says she sees her disenchantment as a kind of metaphor for her whole life – though perhaps that was just jet lag talking.

I told Mason about Jerry's return and Leon's move to San Francisco; he's been trying to reach Leon in Madison for months. Dave Cohen is still working as a carpenter and Peter, who moved up to management in that Heights real estate firm, is thinking about buying a house in Rockaway. I also spoke to Mikey,

who made that Criminal Justice Clinic he's been
wanting to get into.

Last night I went over to Ronna's house to help
Alison with her apartment-hunting. She likes
working at Oxford University Press (imagine a
company that's 500 years old), and I gave her the
suggestion that she'll probably be better off living in
Manhattan; she doesn't like the long commute to
Canarsie and has been taking Dramamine before
going on the subway every day.

Alison knows nothing about neighborhoods, so I told
her that basically, she has the choice between Murray
Hill (within walking distance of work), Chelsea and
the Upper West Side. We had tea and watched *The
Paper Chase* (the TV show). I told her she shouldn't
leave the door unlocked, as she had it when I walked
in. (Barbara was on a date; Billy was at his
grandparents'; Mrs. C was in San Francisco on
business; and Ronna, of course, is still in
Pennsylvania).

This afternoon I drove into Manhattan, and at the
Baronet saw Woody Allen's *Interiors*. Starkly
pessimistic, very Bergmanesque, the film sometimes
falls victim to its own seriousness and seems rather
pretentious. (Some of those lines the actors deliver
about their emotional angst evoked titters in the
audience.)

By making the only vibrant character a vulgar widow, Allen seems to be saying that it's better *not* to be an intellectual or a sensitive person. God, though I admire his attempting a serious art film about creative, neurotic, doomed people – I just think he went overboard in eliminating all traces of humor.

I have a sensibility similar to Woody Allen's, and if I have any role model, it's he. I think that I'd love to – that I *have* to – eventually write a novel akin to Allen's films, or those of Mazursky. But to do that, I need to experience more of life. I cannot write about the present until I have transcended it and become, in some way, a different person.

Monday, September 11, 1978

5 PM. I haven't been called by anyone at Kingsborough, so it looks as though I'll have to hope that LIU comes up with two courses for me.

I got a letter from the chair of the English Department at SUNY Albany; apparently I misunderstood him and there will be no fellowship money available for the spring. So unless some other scholarship comes through, I would have to take out a student loan, which is something I am afraid of doing. It would be *so* much money and very difficult to pay back. Mom says I should just declare bankruptcy like so many others, but I'm not sure that makes me feel very comfortable. I might not be able to get credit or loans if I did that.

So, as of now, I'm up in the air about going to Albany. My parents and friends will probably see my wavering as a failure of nerve, and perhaps it is. Oh I don't know. . . These are difficult times or me, and a good night's sleep, like last night's, is a blessing. I feel I'm in danger of becoming unglued.

I got this really snotty rejection letter from an editor who claimed that my type hurt his eyes – the same type I used on *Disjointed Fictions*. I feel like a failure sometimes.

So, to balance the scale, here's a letter I got from Wesley Strick today: "Just a note to say that my father lent me your material. I'm now sifting through the stories, laughing knowingly (albeit nervously) and (discreetly) dropping your name to my closest friends. The moment I've finished, I'll get in touch. If you can manage that longest of journeys into Manhattan (*vide* Podhoretz, *Making It*), I look forward to meeting with you."

Even if nothing comes of it (and I fully expect nothing will), I am cheered by that note and would be interested in meeting Wesley, whom I am sure is more polished than I could ever be.

Last night I found myself writing poetry; the material didn't seem to come out in fiction. I dreamed of Shelli living in Oregon and coming to visit me with Arthur Bergman, a classmate I hardly knew and whom I haven't thought of in years. The past seems to be closing in on me.

On Saturday at Rockaway, I thought of the Rosh Hashona weekend I spent there ten years ago while we were painting the house. I still have photos of myself on the beach and the terrace taken on that occasion. I remember a terrible anxiety attack I had at night trying to walk across the street to visit Grandma Sylvia. I had a scarf on, one of those things that was popular then, and I abandoned it in the gutter.

Ten years ago I woke up on a Monday morning and decided – out of fear – that I couldn't begin college as scheduled. I've never felt so haunted by the past. Maybe I shouldn't dwell on it, but I need to get in touch with my 1968 seventeen-year-old self. (I have a tissue in my mouth as I write this – what a revolting habit.)

This morning I thought of my sociology prof, Katayama, telling us, "To be free means to be an intellectual. And to be an intellectual means to pay the price of loneliness." He urged me to become a sociologist, said I had a social scientist's mind.

I have a perverse mind. I wrote a bad review of *Disjointed Fictions* under an assumed name (Vivian Sarrett) and submitted it to various magazines.

It's been two weeks since I've seen Ronna, and I don't know if it matters. I miss her, but I can't keep insisting she call me, the way Susan does with her.

Tuesday, September 12, 1978

9 PM. The last day has brought so many changes. Oscar Miller from Kingsborough called at 7:30 last night, while I was at Carolyn Bennett's to bring her my book and some information on the Fiction Collective she needed for an article. Mom called me at the Bennetts', and I phoned Oscar, who gave me a course – English 11B13G, a remedial class that meets from 3 PM – 4 PM every day except Friday.

I got to Kingsborough early today, at 1 PM, wearing a sport jacket despite the warmth. Oscar (he calls me Richard, so I can call him Oscar) told me about the class and gave me a lowdown on what I am to do with them.

Essentially the class is made up of those who passed the CUNY reading test but failed the CUNY writing test. I went to Evelyn, the departmental secretary, and got a roll book, copies of the texts and a whole bunch of forms to fill out. I need my transcripts and three letters of recommendation, but I can get those.

I was having trouble finding my way around the campus, but I finally got to Personnel and filled out a W-4 form. Then I met with my class, in one of the old temporary buildings. They had just come from their mandatory lab section.

The class is all very young and mostly white; they were pretty confused for their first day of class, and I was more than a little confused myself. But the class went well except for the fact that so many of them are pissed that they had to be in Remedial in the first place.

Back at the English Department, which had just had a meeting, I waited for over an hour, watching the chaos, until I had persevered so long that Oscar relented and gave me another course – a 23, the second sequence of the remedial track, that meets every day but Thursday from 12:40-1:40 PM. I'll see them tomorrow.

Exhausted after being bombarded by so many new experiences, I came home to supper and a hot bath. Kingsborough pays $22 an hour, so I'll be making about $150-$176 a week, depending on holidays. That's almost twice as much as I made at LIU.

Now comes the dilemma: Should I take a course at
LIU this fall? I wouldn't take two, but if I could get a
class between 9-10 AM or 10-11 AM, I might do it. It
will mean more work than I'm used to, but I'm afraid
to let my connection with LIU to slip. Kingsborough
might not hire me next term and then where will I be?
(Not in Albany – I guess this decides *that*.)

Oh well, I will have time to think about it. Maybe I
should work harder – but then I'm afraid I won't have
time for my writing. The first three days of the week
I'll be at KCC (I'll use that abbreviation from here on
in) from about noon until 4 PM, and I need time to
write, exercise, dawdle, and be lazy.

This seems very unreal; a week ago it seemed
impossible. I've been so comfortable at LIU and it's
difficult for me to adjust to KCC – but it's probably
good for me psychologically. Everyone in the
department seems fairly nice, but there are so many
faces, I can't keep their names straight. I still have to
get my ID card and parking sticker. Whew!

As I said, I was at Carolyn's last night; *she* is so
incredibly busy that I'm in awe of her organization.
It's nice to have a neighbor I can discuss the small-
press scene with.

Grandma Ethel and Grandpa Herb came by after
going to the hospital. The doctor told Grandma Ethel

that she's improved slightly but it will take a lot of time.

I got sent a xerox copy of my Joanne Vicente article in *The People's Almanac 2*, out in October. "R.G." is given credit and my name appears on the contributors' page.

Wednesday, September 13, 1978

7 PM. These are very stressful times for me. I was wide-awake last night, trying to decide what to do about LIU. I finally decided that I'm not going to take any courses there. Monetarily, the benefits would be about $35 extra a week, and at KCC I'm till earning $1,100 more than I would be at LIU.

I remember how unhappy I was when I was teaching, coordinating the BC publishing conference, working for the Fiction Collective and trying to find time to write. Both courses I'm teaching are unfamiliar to me, and I have to prepare 8 one-hour class lessons a week – plus mark a lot of papers.

In a way I dread leaving LIU the same way I couldn't tear myself away from Brooklyn College when I started the M.A. program at Richmond. I've made many friends at LIU; I'll miss the office coffeeklatsch

and Margaret and my little cubbyhole and the
elevators and lunch at Junior's and everything.

But I must move on. Kingsborough is a different kind
of place – almost all the students are very young,
fresh out of high school, nearly ten years younger
than I. I have to walk a great deal across a real
campus to get to my classes; it's pleasanter than an
elevator but less convenient.

The drive to school is shorter at KCC, and I paid $5
for my parking permit today. I also got my ID and
my mailbox; my office will be C305, right near the
English Department. None of the professors talk to
me, but none of them did at LIU at first – it took me
several terms to get to know them.

Fall is really here. It's dark now and it's quite chilly.
I feel very much like the kid who started Brooklyn
College nine years ago. I can understand how hard it
is for my students to adjust. I have made only one
friend, another adjunct, Anna Bono.

My English 23 students seemed very hostile and very
bored. I tried, but I could reach only a few of them.
I'm going to have to help them with reading
comprehension and I've never done that before.
Anyway, it seems I have enough to do without taking
on another course at LIU.

Now that Taplinger is interested in doing a book, I need time to write and revise my stories. I may be able to move out soon – I've got to decide what I want to do with my life. With my schedule the way it is, I don't have to get up early at all (and tomorrow I don't have to be in school till 3 PM and on Friday I get to leave early, at 1:40 PM).

I am having fun with my English 11 students; we seem to like each other. I gave them an essay to do today: "Who Are You? What Are You Doing Here?" I will have to take some to somebody in charge, as about ten of the students don't think they belong in a remedial course and they certainly write better than those at LIU.

I can't blame them for being upset about taking a 5-hour course for only 2 credits. But it's bad that I have to deal with their resentment. Anyway, I am interested in my classes and I welcome the challenge of teaching them: it's a lot like teaching high school.

Michael Kramer phoned last night, and I promised I'd given in his resume at LIU. He's still feeling ill and has lost 10 pounds – and Michael's so skinny to begin with.

The Helen Review accepted "Complacencies of the Peignoir," my first acceptance of any value in months. Even though it's a one-page "story," I'm glad they

took it. Right now I face difficulty in writing my
name.

Thursday, September 14, 1978

7 PM. Against my better judgment, I took a course at
LIU: English 12, the C hour – 10 AM on Mondays,
Wednesdays and Fridays. I'll have only an hour and
a half to get to my 12:40 PM class at Kingsborough.
God knows when I'll get a chance to write or to
socialize or to live. Hard work *does* scare me.
During my 11 class today, I felt myself slipping out of
my body, that old anxiety-attack feeling. I let it flow
over me, the way Weekes and others say you're
supposed to do, and it passed fairly quickly.

I took the class at LIU because I wanted to. I know
that. Margaret awoke me out of a dream this
morning and I told her I couldn't teach a class from
10 AM to 12 PM. But then I raced over to LIU, giving
Margaret a list of the hours I could be available;
tonight Dr. Tucker called me. I have to rush over for
a meeting after my class at Kingsborough, but I'll
manage.

If I can get through the next two weeks, which will be
very hectic (especially with Dad going in for surgery),
I can get through the term – because the holidays

come up and then midterms and the term at Kingsborough ends before Christmas.

Mondays and Wednesdays will be the worst, with 3 classes from 10 AM to 4 PM. Thursdays will be easy with one class from 3-4 PM. Tuesdays I can sleep late, and on Friday I'll be finished early. But this is my first full-time job and I'm scared.

The fact that I'll be making $3,100 over the next 4 months doesn't excite me because the money isn't real to me yet. Never having had any money of my own, I can't imagine what that kind of salary will mean. I suppose I can manage, and I shouldn't anticipate trouble.

I haven't been writing much anyway lately and maybe I've had too *much* time rather than too little. But I've never worked 5 days a week before, and so much has been thrown at me all at once.

I have sore legs from walking across the campus and a sore throat from teaching, and while I turned my back, summer disappeared – you couldn't go out without a jacket today.

Maybe what scares me is that I'm now actually becoming an adult, fully able to take care of himself. It's overwhelming. I called Alice and she was thrilled that I'm not going to Albany. I spoke to Teresa, who was depressed that her lover, Ray, split for New

Mexico after a big argument – in just six weeks they had become very close.

Bill-Dale replied to my letter with all the intolerant idealism he possesses. He was very turned off by my "cynicism about the '60s" and my pragmatism. His philosophy is very mixed-up, but then, he is 21: "Yes, we do come from two different generations. Yes, you have lost the idealism of youth. I have no desire to see that much of you, but I would still like to see you to interview for the book [his project on bisexuality, obviously some sort of self-justification] . . . The one thing which energizes me is meeting driven, idealistic people. Meeting idealists turned pragmatists (it's 1978 and we're older now, Jerry Rubin's *Growing Up* premise) or '70s apathetic, I can tolerate but I don't go out of the way for. . . Love & strength, Bill-Dale."

Twerp. No, I can't write him off like that. He's just young and I was like him once. Though he hates smugness, he *is* smug – the way we were so self-righteous about everything eight or ten years ago. I think I'll use his three letters as a story. "Portrait of the Idealist as a Young Man" so something, perhaps? I'd include my own letters, but that might make it less interesting. Bill-Dale is looking for a carbon copy of himself, and he'll never find it. (I *know*.)

Yesterday Brad had another ad in the *Voice*: "Love is blind and cannot find me." I wrote him back: "Love may be blind, but I've got contact lenses."

Friday, September 15, 1978

5 PM. I was very upset last evening and finally phoned Martin Tucker and told him I couldn't take the course. He was pissed and said he understood. God knows why I did it that way. My intentions were good, he said as he marched off to the netherworld.

I seem to have trouble, as Mrs. Ehrlich pointed out, moving from one stage of life to the next. I always end up breaking ties in a stupid way (*vide* Baumbach and the Fiction Collective, my therapists, whatever). But now I'm at Kingsborough and I'm happy. I can get an apartment and somehow I'll get the rent paid.

I don't have to drive myself crazy. I can sleep late and have time for writing and enjoying life. Albany is out. Maybe I've fucked things up again – God knows, my parents believe that and they disapprove of my decision – but this is what I'm comfortable with.

The extra $675 just wasn't worth it to me. To feel relaxed, as I do now, for the first time all week, is worth a great deal more. I'll still be making over $2100 for the term, more money than I've ever earned, and I have a real job.

I am becoming adjusted to Kingsborough – today I found my office a lovely room overlooking the first floor where the students congregate, with my own phone extension and a filing cabinet and room to move around in.

My 23 class went very well today. I have their trust now, and I'm really looking forward to the term. So if I've fucked things up, I'm ending up feeling pretty happy. I don't feel oppressed now and I'm as comfortable in my classrooms as I ever was – maybe even more so. (I think it has something to do with a more fluid environment; things are looser than at LIU.)

And I'll be able to bring in money. Yesterday a check for $25 arrived from *The Mississippi Mud*, part of their CCLM grant.

Today is a cool, dark, drizzly day, a perfect day to end the week, a day you can get lost in. Oh, maybe last night had something to do with Bill-Dale's letter; I woke up I the middle of the night feeling angry at him. Who is he to judge me? He's 21 and I was 21 in 1972 and probably just as smart and snot-nosed as he is. God, can young people be so pompous and self-righteous and intolerant!

When I was 21, I knew everything. Of course I'd never worked a day in my life. I know I haven't had a hard time of it, but since then I did work for $2 an hour shelving books in the library and being a messenger and a department store clerk (all while I had a masters degree) and after I had *two* masters degrees I worked in a nursing home.

Of course I've had an easy life, but I've seen more of life than Bill-Dale Bonhoffer has. He makes the Sixties his god; well, I prefer to live in the present, whether that means the Seventies or the Eighties or the Nineties (what do they call the first decade of the new century anyway? The Single Numbers?).

Anyway, I've discovered that 21-year-olds are less mature than I am. Do I feel smug? No. Bill-Dale is the one with all the answers – love, magic, V-signs. No wonder Kent State and the Chicago convention police riot happened: even though the young people (we) were right, we were insufferable about being right.

So I'm a bit too cynical, a bit too superior (my worst stories are those in which I feel superior to my characters). Give me time: I'm sure that the older I get, the more unsure of myself I will be.

Saturday, September 16, 1978

8 PM. I am feeling comfortable with myself. I like the way I look, and even if I'm a fuck-up, I do seem to be doing all right. Elaine Taibi called yesterday to say that she was looking through a stack of *Flatbush Lifes*

when she found the article about me. She liked
"Hitler" and found it very moving. She and Maddy
Berg were trying to think up a way to get me into the
Alumni Bulletin without my knowing it; they're
under the mistaken assumption that I'm modest.
Well, publicly I am – very. I can't take
accomplishment well – like all narcissists, I really
don't like myself all that much and want all my praise
to come from myself.

I went out to dinner at the Floridian, and when I
returned, Brad called. "I said I'd call you after Labor
Day," he told me. "I just didn't say *which* Labor Day."
Brad reminded me that we've known each other over
9 years "although we've probably had 27 minutes of
conversation in all that time."

He put the ad in the *Voice* because Danny has gone
away to Dartmouth, and though their relationship
had lasted for two and a half years (an incredibly long
time, to my way of thinking), it was time to move on.

Brad can't stand the thought of being alone; he's
really a very conservative homebody. In fact, he's
going to move out of Manhattan when his lease
expires next year (he doesn't really take advantage of
the Manhattan nightlife, and 14th Street I becoming
very seedy).

He's still Brad, still playing the big brother, concerned
about growing old, very practical but melodramatic.

Anyway, we said we'd get together one of these days
– which probably means 1980.

I picked Alice up at 7:30 PM, just when she and her
mother were about to have one of their usual sessions.
Alice is leaving for Europe in a couple of weeks and
her mother's following her in early October; Kat will
be provided for by a trio of good-natured friends who
will alternate feeding days.

Alice, on the drive downtown, told me that she's
having fights with Philip and even began responding
to *Voice* ads again. We were a bit afraid to get out by
the church on Willoughby Ave., but finally we did
and went upstairs as Charlene Victor, the very down-
to-earth culture czar of Brooklyn, was extolling the
virtues of the Downtown Cultural Center and Janice
and her co-coordinator.

We saw a scene from a playwriting workshop, some
simulated acting lessons, heard a jazz group, and
downstairs we looked at the paintings and sculpture.
Dolores Rosamine was there, looking as strong and
vibrant as ever – and Harry Steinberg the
pornographer and hack writer – and Richard Rutner,
Janice's painter friend who administers the Visual
Arts program out in Hempstead.

I spoke to all of them and to some calligraphers (one
woman told me she's known Louis Strick for years
and "he does things that lose money, just for the love

of it"). Janice showed us her resumé, which lists me and Alice as references!

The spirit of that place is something to see – there's a great deal of energy there. I wish I was poor enough to apply for a CETA job so I could teach writing in a place like that.

I took Alice back into Manhattan and we stopped at the Eighth Street Bookshop – where I found *Disjointed Fictions* right in the front of their window! I was exultant. I felt, as I drove home to Brooklyn, that I had conquered New York. I'm in love with this city, its energy and diversity and I don't want to leave. Like the TV commercials say, I love New York.

I got home just in time to see the final rounds of the Ali-Spinks rematch and to see Ali crowned heavyweight champ for the third time. I think he's the greatest man in America today – at 36, to keep fighting. In the spring I was sickened by his defeat, but last night his victory gave me new hope. I just hope he gives up boxing for good now.

This afternoon Josh and I went to a very crowded poetry reading and heard John Ashbery and Michael Lally. We couldn't get seats and we couldn't even see them, so we left early.

Sunday, September 17, 1978

8 PM. It's been a terrific weekend and it's too bad it has to end. But I don't have to get up early in the morning and that's a blessing.

I spent most of the day with Ronna. I didn't realize how much I missed her until I saw her. She looked terrific, thinner than I've ever known her to be. I walked in while she was drying her hair.

Alison, who was at Mass, finally decided to take an apartment in Canarsie, a few blocks from Ronna's house. Ronna's sister loves her job at the health clinic in the Bronx and is seeing a guy she works with who lives in Rockaway.

Ronna and I drove out to Long Island on the Interboro, Grand Central and Northern State; as we drove, we talked about we've been doing. And Ronna told me about her friend Pat in University Park, and Phil the smelly British weightlifter and how her grandmother stopped talking to all her relatives over invitations to various affairs.

We walked around the mall in Roosevelt Field and had lunch in Lum's (Ollieburgers), discussing life in academia. Her job at Metro is basically a bimmie position, but it's a holding action; things should go better when Susan returns from Europe. (Susan, incidentally, does not think that badly of me, and John Richards actually likes me a lot).

Marvin keeps trying to set Ronna up with his friends but that's mostly sublimation; also, he'll feel more secure with Susan if Ronna's paired off with a guy.

Back at my house, we made love – it was very sweet. I'm crazy about Ronna that way; I like making her feel good. She wonders sometimes if it's wise of us to continue to have a physical relationship, but there's no reason *not* to: it doesn't stop either of us from looking elsewhere.

And I only feel possessive when we're alone in bed; otherwise I've managed not to be jealous. Today she was telling me about the guy in Middletown who was married and how she used to ride with him on his motorcycle to Hershey.

I love Ronna as though she were my sister. I suppose it's naïve to say that and undoubtedly it will all backfire one day but for now our relationship is working well. I am gay, after all – or that's the excuse I give for not allowing myself to get hurt with her.

I say "I love you" to Ronna but she doesn't reciprocate; still, she makes it clear how she feels about me. One thing she can't stand is my pomposity and self-importance about my work, but today she

said she's beginning to think that all things I say
about myself are true.

Yesterday's reading was a bust, but it did inspire me
to write some prose poems last night. I think I've
found a form that suits what I've been trying to say of
late. I have a renewed confidence in my work.

Yesterday *The Westbere Review* took "In The Sixties,"
one of my better pieces, and that plus the *Helen
Review* acceptance, seeing *The People's Almanac 2*
piece, and getting a check from *The Mississippi Mud* all
make me feel that I still have it.

Actually, things are going so well, I'm almost
terrified. What payments will Fate make in return for
all this? Next week is Dad's surgery and I'm trying
not to think too much about it. I supposes *he*'s doing
the same thing. Avis sent a postcard from the Côte de
Azur, where she, Helmut and Heinz are sunning
themselves, eating delicious French meals and getting
the summer that missed Bremen this year.

The past week has turned out to be one of the nicest
of the year: only good things seemed to happen. I feel
lucky and I know this can't last so I'm going to enjoy
it while I can.

I've got to call George now – he sent me a letter about
my helping him teach creative writing to Harrisburg
high school kids one weekend in November.

Monday, September 18, 1978

7 PM. I'm very glad I decided not to teach at LIU. I would have been a total wreck if I had to run around so much. I only spend about 4 hours at Kingsborough, true, but they are smack in the middle of the day and I relish the spare time I have on either side of classes.

My 23 class is very dense and they can't seem to adjust to having such a young teacher. One woman in particular, a nursing student, gave me a rough time. At LIU my whiteness made me stand out and so my age didn't seem very much of a factor. At Kingsborough I look undistinguishable from most of the students.

I heard one guy say that he could teach the class; it looks a lot easier than it is, of course. But anyway, this is *their* problem, not mine. After teaching for almost 4 years, I've got no hang-ups about being in front of the classroom. I'm getting paid well enough so that I can stand my students' obnoxiousness – and they can get a surprise when their final grade comes.

I planned out most of my week's lessons, but there's still more preparation to be done. Things will get easier after these two weeks when we have four holidays in the next two weeks. By then I should be used to them and they should be used to me.

Stephen Sponk told me that Elihu's teaching a course at LIU and has an assistantship at CUNY – good for him. I still don't really have any friends at KCC yet, but maybe I don't need any. (Oh, come off it, Grayson: one can always use friends.)

I called George last night, a woman answered, and I think I'd interrupted something. I told George I'd come into Harrisburg on Thursday, November 9 and help him teach creative writing to "the cream of the crop" of Pennsylvania creative writing students at a conference at the Host Inn (it's sponsored by the State Press Association).

 I'll only have to cancel one class, and it should be fun; besides, it will look good on my resumé. (Speaking of resumés, I got a letter from Neil Schaeffer thanking me for my "fine" one and saying he was sorry that there were no jobs at BC.)

George told me he'll be coming in three weeks for the Book Fair, to be held this year at the Martin Luther King High School across from Lincoln Center. I told him he could stay here or possibly at one of my Manhattan friends' apartments.

Last night President Carter announced that the Camp David summit had ended with an agreement on basic

principles between Egypt and Israel. A final peace
treaty is months away, if it ever comes (and there are
rumblings that it might not), but it was thrilling to see
President Sadat and Prime Minister Begin hugging
each other and pledging friendship. And certainly
this can only help Carter with his popularity
problems.

Today was a humid, drizzly day, very uncomfortable.
I worked on sending out submissions after I got home
from school; there doesn't seem to be enough time to
work on my stories and poetry.

Suddenly I feel I have nothing more to write, and that
scares and frustrates me. Other days I could write
dozens of pages, maybe even a novel. Is it just that
nothing's happening or am I numbed to things? Or,
even worse, am I repressing something?

Let's play a game. (Why not? I have a dozen lines
left.) If I were an animal today, I'd be a whooping
crane. If I were a color, I'd be sky blue. If I were a
planet, I'd be Mercury. If I were a novel, I'd be *Cold
Comfort Farm*. If I were a food, I'd be strawberry jello
(as in J.D. Salinger's quote, "where there's smoke,
there's usually strawberry jello"). If I were a piece of
furniture, I'd be a rocking chair. If I were a state, I'd
be Kansas. If I were a President, I'd be Benjamin
Harrison. If I were a drink, I'd be Kool-Aid. If I were
a poet, I'd be Mayakovsky. If I were a baseball team,
I'd be the Oakland Athletics.

And what does all this say about my present state of mind? I'd rather not know. (I *must* be depressing.) Maybe I'll analyze this in a week or a year and a half from now.

Tuesday, September 19, 1978

5 PM. I think what I was feeling last night was dissatisfaction. My 23 class is so immature I can hardly get through a lesson with them. They interrupt, giggle, make silly noises – I've never had such a bad class. I understand now that the "C.C." after Kingsborough stands for Country Club rather than Community College for most students. It's a glorified extension of high school.

The 11 students have just come in and so they don't understand the system yet; I can deal with them more effectively. Of course I'm not going to let the students get to me; I'm getting paid $22 an hour regardless of whether they learn anything or not. But they are so *stupid*! They can't make simple cognitive leaps of understand, and like most stupid people, they think they know everything. I will fail some of them with satisfaction when the term ends.

Last night and during my office hour today I thought a great deal about college teaching; I'm not sure I want to make a career out of it. Even when I finally get to teach fiction writing, I'm sure I'll have to spend most of my efforts correcting grammatical mistakes. Literacy has declined to such shocking levels that I believe it's the number-one problem for America's future.

I get no satisfaction from the enormous sense of superiority I feel vis-à-vis most people: Who is going to be around to read anything I write? Even a very bright young man like Bill-Dale makes mistakes (his apostrophes on plurals, for example) that my fourth grade teacher would have reprimanded me for.

And I've begun to spot errors like "the team lost it's [sic] first game" in magazines like *Time* and *Newsweek* – and even on our Kingsborough schedule form we are told where to find the "Admission's" office. God. Our heroes today are dumb and inarticulate – Travolta, the Fonz – whereas '50s idols like Brando and James Dean were *bright* and inarticulate.

Anyway, what does this all mean for me? Well, maybe I should get out of college teaching and get into something more intellectual. I might enjoy an office job like Alison's in a citadel of literacy like Oxford University Press. Office work means a 9-to-5 day, but at least you're not "on" all the time as you are when you teach.

I'm going to look around for a job, and in December, when the term ends, I'm going to attempt to get a job outside academia. I enjoyed working in the Fiction Collective office and maybe I could get something that challenging again.

This morning I stood on line at the bank behind a guy who just sold his business (three record stores) for $250,000 – and he wasn't much older than me. Now he intends to "retire" for a couple of years and concentrate on a travel agency, which he runs for the sheer pleasure of it.

The more money I earn, the more important money becomes to me. Richard Sasano's writing PR for Resorts International seems no less noble than trying to teach sentence structure to idiots. Why should I keep banging my head against the wall?

Academia is as stifling as advertising; at least Kingsborough and LIU are. After four years, maybe it's time to call it quits. I can always go back when I'm more established as a writer and get the brightest classes.

It's dark and chilly out. Our paychecks will come on October 20 and that will make me feel a little better – but not all that much.

Wednesday, September 20, 1978

8 PM. Surprisingly, I feel very sexy tonight. I looked at myself in the mirror and I saw a handsome face –

round and a bit chubby but good-looking. I started
using a roll-on deodorant rather than a spray, and
somehow that feels more sensuous. I've got new
short sleeved shirts and since the summer I've been
wearing colored bikini briefs instead of the dull white
ones. My beard has gotten thicker and darker and
I'm even getting some more hair on my chest.

One thing I suppose I haven't written about
Kingsborough is that it's given me a chance to look at
some gorgeous guys about 17-19. I must pass fifty
guys a day that I'm attracted to. That doesn't bother
or frustrate me at all; it *does* make me feel very alive.

Yesterday was a bad day and so I had complaints;
today was a good day and I feel great about teaching.
I asserted myself with the 23 class today and we had a
pretty good discussion on the reading, an essay on
capital punishment.

Ms. Cordero, the Puerto Rican woman, still bursts out
laughing every time she sees me, but she's not an
idiot. (There are more than a few in the class – people
who must be actual morons.)

She told the class about her cousin, who drowned his
little boy in the Narrows a few weeks ago. He went
out with the child and returned without him. When
his family became frantic, he said he'd take them to
him; he stopped by the Verrazano Bridge and pointed
into the bay. "He's at the bottom now," he told them.

And he had previously killed three of his other children! What kind of monsters live in this world? The class was of course horrified by this story, but Ms. Cordero takes it calmly. Her cousin has spent time in Kings County Hospital but is out often, and this time the judge dismissed charges against him. I would like to learn more about this incident; I just can't imagine such a thing happening.

My 11 class was good because I had a brainstorm. We went over an essay in the third person and I decided to split the class into pairs and let them interview each other and then write a paragraph about each other. It worked, and they were pretty enthusiastic; one of them even interviewed me. I'll read them out loud tomorrow and go over their errors. I enjoyed teaching today, and my week is three-quarters over – just one class tomorrow and Friday.

Alice sent me a Polaroid snapshot of *Disjointed Fictions* in the window of the Eighth Street Bookshop. I called Alice to thank her and she said Andreas had taken it on the weekend, when they found Laura sitting out front on her break, smoking a joint. Laura even rearranged the window so they could get a good shot; she has the book on display upstairs too. God, I have such nice friends.

I called Mason, and he's having a devil of a time with his junior high students. They're as wild as anything, won't let him teach, and they won't give him a break.

Mason has such a hard time asserting himself and
he's still got all of his '60s ideas of progressive,
"open" education.

Well, if he's to survive – and he's already thought
about quitting – Mason's got to act tough and not give
the little monsters an inch. I told Mason we should
both emulate John Houseman as dictatorial law Prof.
Kingsfield on *The Paper Chase* (now a TV show).

This evening I went to visit Grandpa Herb and
Grandma Ethel, whose cousin Rose Levine (Dave
Tarras's daughter) died today, at 53. Poor Uncle
Dave and Aunt Shifra.

Grandma showed me the lengthy questionnaire that
nutrition doctor gave her. It covers *everything* – not
only about herself but her parents and siblings. (She
was told that her mother died at 29 of "malnutrition"
and doesn't know much more than that.)

Grandma Ethel had to write down everything she ate
all week. She had Arlyne help her with the
questionnaire. I noticed that Grandma's periods
began at 14 and ended at 45 and she didn't check the
box about whether her sex life was satisfactory.
Grandma Ethel did check "depressed," "jumpy" and
"worried" but not "irritable," which sounds about
right.

Thursday, September 21, 1978

7 PM. Just a couple of hours before the official beginning of autumn, yet summer is still with us. It was hot and sunny and humid today; there's really no need for it now, though.

Dad and Mom went to see his surgeon today. Dad enters Brookdale on Sunday, with the operation scheduled for Monday morning. I think Mom wanted me to take off from work, but Marc will be with her, and there's not anything I can do at the hospital. Working will help keep me occupied during the long (5-hour) and intricate surgery.

Dad's pretty frightened, as he should be. I've tried to keep from upsetting him any further. Like him, I just wish it was all over and we knew the tumor was benign.

I went to Kingsborough at 2:45 this afternoon, just pulling up to the T-4 building in time for my 3 PM class. I had a delightful time as I read the students' essays about one another – and I turned it into a clinic of writing problems. I get along well with the 11 class; I just wish I had the same rapport with the other class.

I haven't been writing much this week, but I've been submitting a great deal; I used up almost $15 worth of stamps. I've been trying to submit a bit more shrewdly, using skill in matching the story to the publication.

Sue Stephens of *Tailings*, who had previously accepted my "Conjectures" and "The Fiction Writer and His Friends" sent me a Xeroxed letter asking for submissions for a "mini-chapbook" of 12-16 pages. I sent along a lot of material for her to consider.

I'd really like to concentrate on books now. Richard Meade of the Story Press of Chicago sent a delightful letter, saying he'd love to do a collection, but it's dependent upon a number of things, including grants on a return on the investment for their original books (including one by V.S. Pritchett).

I wrote back, encouraging him to keep me in mind a year from now; it can't hurt to have a back-up system in case Taplinger falls through. (I'm getting annoyed that I haven't heard from either of the Stricks in nearly two weeks.)

SUNY-Albany's financial aid director wrote me that there's no work/study money for the spring, and even their NDSL loans are filled up. So – I'm not going to Albany and that settles it. I just can't afford it. Well, that's one reason.

David Gross wrote me from Bath, Maine. I feel I never got back to him the weekend he was here for his brother's wedding. He went to Bread Loaf again

and was in Gilmore again. There was a party with
girls at the house every night:

"We had one wild poet who was going to hold a
'Worst Poetry' conference, but he left after the first
week. I chose Gardner again as my Reader. He told
me that I had ironed out all the mechanical problems
that I had in '77, but all the excitement of the novel
had been drained. He said it was 'dull.' Maybe that
reflects my life up here in Maine. I'm still working in
my father's factory, so a lot of my energy goes to
recuperating from 9 hours of walking on the ole feet."

David says the food and weather were better this year
at Bread Loaf, though *The Crumb* wasn't as funny.
And much of the instruction was repetitious, so
David won't return again. He's decided to shelve his
novel ("I did learn one cold fact – actually it was
rubbed in my face: No matter who you work with,
your name doesn't mean anything until you are
published.") He sent me a pretty good story and I
wrote him back with suggestions.

Friday, September 22, 1978

3 PM. Mom took the keys to Marc's rented car last
night and Marc had to go out. I lent him my car and I
took the bus to Brooklyn College. It wasn't so bad.
I'm the only one in this family who doesn't think he's

too good for public transportation. And the feeling that I can get there from here is a good one; it keeps me from getting scared.

Last night (it was dark by 7:30) was warm, and the campus looked so empty. (Later I discovered that enrollment is down to 19,000 as compared to 35,000 when I was an undergraduate.)

The Alumni Board of Directors meetings are a bore and we always get off on tangents that go nowhere, but it's good to see old and familiar faces. And the tea and cakes are always first-rate.

Elaine Taibi was pleased that I gave her a few stories to read. She asked if she could get my book at the Eighth Street, and I was pleased to say yes. She asked Ira Harkavy if he'd read "Hitler" in *Flatbush Life* and Ira, always the politician (he thinks I'm an eccentric), said he did.

Maddy Bergman and Peter Rosen came up from the Executive Board meeting and we said hello. Maddy is finding the second year of law school just as much work as the first. She told me the deadline for Class Notes is October 15 – something else for me to do. Oh well, somebody's got to do it; it's my third year on the job and I suppose I enjoy being the recorder of other people's lives.

Jerry Borenstein told me he was surprised that the Anniversarygrams netted $3800 so far, which is better than he expected. He urged me to write to Irwin Shaw, who's a lovely man, he says – as well as a heavy drinker.

Peter Rosen is married to Joanne Decker, they live in Flushing (where "politics is dull") and he still works as counsel to the Major League Baseball Players Association.

Mike Isaacs came in late because he teaches a class in Advanced Personality at Queens College on Tuesdays and Thursdays; he's pleased he got the job on his own. He left the program at Fordham after a dispute with the new chairman, who's very conservative; Mike would now like to get into the CUNY Graduate Center.

Eddie Wasserman, looking every inch the young lawyer in his three-piece gray flannel suit, is working for a downtown law firm. Wells Barron, who got heavy again, is going for his M.A. in Poli Sci at BC and has just come off several losing political campaigns, including Bloom's for governor. We talked about local politics and the losses of Balter and Kravitz and the victories of Rhoda Jacobs and Marty Markowitz.

At the meeting we approved the budget, some new constitutional amendments, got into a ridiculously protracted debate (as usual) and heard the report on CUNY – it may be absorbed into SUNY, but by now nobody really cares as long as BC continues to be a good school.

The meeting broke up at 10 PM and I got a lift with Wells, who also drove Eddie home; we chatted about this one and that one, who's where and who married whom. Eddie mentioned running into Alex Smith, so I assume that he knows that Lorna died. (Was it five years ago that he and Lorna double-dated with Ronna and me?)

I had some news that Ronna had given me earlier: Sid and Carole are getting married in June. Carole is finishing her fiction dissertation at IU and Sid's enrolled in an Urbanology program at Antioch.

I told my parents that I had to take the bus home. That was terrible, but I wanted to play the martyr.

Today I taught singular and plural in English 23 and did a good job. I got six rejections today and I tried to write but didn't get very far. It's a dark, cool, humid day. Tonight I'm going out but I wish I was staying in.

Saturday, September 23, 1978

6 PM. Autumn came in cool – it's hard to get around without wearing a jacket. I've just been sitting at the counter of the Arch, chewing on a cheeseburger and playing with a tossed salad and apprising myself of my shortcomings as a human being, writer and son – mostly the latter.

Dad is checking into Brookdale at 1 PM tomorrow and his surgery is scheduled for sometime on Monday. As much as we believe everything will turn out all right, it's foolish not to recall that things don't always work out for the best.

My father's life for the past six or seven years has been a continuous and unrelenting series of disappointments and it pains me to think that I have become one of them. I know Dad would say, "That's ridiculous; none of my children are a disappointment to me." But since I've never been a father and I've never been *my* father, I find that difficult to believe.

I've been so disappointed in *him* and didn't I let him know it. I can be very harsh in my judgments, telling Dad that he's behaving counterproductively or negatively and that's why things always go wrong for him. Of course I am a great psychologist, having come to the stage of well-adjustment through 8 years of therapy (which he *paid for* – $10,000 worth, a sum that could open up a door or two for him now – but he never begrudges me for it).

I never did accept him for himself; I always tried to make him The Perfect Father. These things don't make me feel very good about myself. Oh, I know, I know: at times like this everyone is feeling vaguely guilty for the moment, but that doesn't change how I feel, does it?

I haven't said "I love you" to him since I-don't-know-when. I take his generosity as a matter of course. I look at him from time to time with disapproval and bemusement. Not a model son. And the worst of is he's two rooms away lying on the floor watching a college football game and as much a I may want to walk in there and hug him, I can't. Sad. Maybe I can and maybe I will – later.

I just wish life could turn around for him and not start picking up speed downhill as it did with Uncle Morty and Uncle Abe. My father has had termites of suffering for years and I don't know if I can bear to see things get worse for him. (This is the closest I've come to unselfishness in a long while.)

Saturday evening. Autumn. The 23rd of September. It's been over two months since I've written anything first-rate and I know it. Let's face it: the Courier-Life article; the publication of the chapbook; the jobs at

LIU and Kingsborough; the feelers from Taplinger – none of this has done my writing any good.

I've been merely repeating tired themes and overused formulae. That's why I spent hours and money today sending out over 30 submissions – I'm desperate. The more outwardly I show success, the greater my feelings of failure.

This page may be the most *real* writing I've done in weeks. Every word aches as it comes out of the pen and spills neatly on this page. I know nothing about myself or other people or any of this, so why don't I shut up?

Or else: Last night Mason and I drove to Manhattan in the rain. We picked up Mikey and then Mason's (and Shelli's) friend Debbie, who's unhappily working at Paragon because she can't get a job designing for a theater.

We ate at Emilio's on Sixth Avenue (at my suggestion) and then we couldn't figure out what to do. There were no parking spaces uptown and I acted like an extroverted maniac, yelling at people, making the others laugh. Eventually we sat in the West 80th Street apartment Debbie shares with Nancy Corigliano, Marie's sister, doing very little but sitting and listening to Jackson Browne.

Sunday, September 24, 1978

4 PM. A few hours ago we drove over to Brookdale Hospital in my car; I let Dad drive because he felt it would steady his nerves. We were lucky enough to get a nearby parking space, and we checked into Admissions. There we waited for a long time before Dad's name was called.

I went in with him to be interviewed about his medical insurance, he signed some consent forms, and paid $5 for a phone. They had his address wrong, leaving out the zero in '1607,' so the forms had to be done over. Then he went for a blood test, a urinanalysis and an EKG.

Aunt Sydelle surprised us in the lobby; a friend had driven her from Cedarhurst. We all went up to Dad's room, on a new floor, and I left them there. Mom wants to stay there all the time, and there's no reasoning with her; I think Dad is comforted by the way she hovers.

He didn't seem nervous, though I know how frightened he must be. I hugged and kissed him goodbye and said, "I love you." I still don't know what time surgery is scheduled for. Being in the hospital made me very tense; my arms and legs began to ache and I felt a tension headache beginning. I'm very nervous, but that's natural.

I plan to teach tomorrow, as there's nothing I can do at the hospital. Mom and Marc will be there, and so will Grandma Ethel and Grandpa Herb. I think Jonny's afraid of even visiting a hospital; he's got all these neurotic fears and hypochondria that I once had. Last night he didn't want Donna in his room because she mentioned that she'd vomited the day before. Thank God (*God?*) I don't have that mishigass anymore.

There's really nothing to be done now except wait. I don't pray because even if there was a God, He couldn't make a benign tumor malignant or vice versa. We can hope, that's all, Dad having a malignancy would be against the odds, but he's had a lot of bad breaks.

But I can't think about that now; I *won't*; I don't have to wonder about that possibility now. Besides, even if it's benign, there could be complications – an infection or whatever. This is the most serious operation a member of the immediate family has had, and I hope we have the strength to get through it.

Aunt Sydelle said she'd tell Grandma Sylvia that Dad was out of town on business, but Mom told her not to say anything; maybe Dad can call her Tuesday night. We're all going to be under a great deal of stress this week.

Surprisingly, I've been writing a little – and it's not all
that bad, either. I slept soundly when I did sleep,
though I kept waking up every few hours. I phoned
Ronna, who was helping Alison clean up her new
apartment. I can't write another word now.

*

9 PM. We just came back from the hospital. I went
with Marc and Donna at 6:30. Jonny was lifting
weights and said he "couldn't be ready" in time. I
know he wanted to see Dad, but his terror prevented
him, and now is not the time to make an issue of it.

We found Dad in his pajamas and bathrobe, and
Mom by his side. The five of us sat in the dayroom.
Dad looked pale, but then so did I. It was a moment
of drama, but I can't relate it as I would in a story
because it's not a story. Dad said, "You should be
able to get a story out of this." Maybe someday.

We made the kind of absurd small talk and ridiculous
jokes that you make to keep from screaming. Donna,
with her naiveté, really helped. The anesthesiologist
came and talked to Dad; he's scheduled for surgery a
8 AM.

Dad said he's been in hospital rooms all his life and
it's a shock to him when he looks down and sees the
bathrobe and the wrist bracelet. I can't imagine what
he's going through. It was very poignant to leave him

there. Tomorrow we'll know if it's malignant or benign: two words and one means a future and the other means. . .

Monday, September 25, 1978

5 PM. Benign. But I can't seem to say "benign" without "thank God." "Thank God" is what I said when I first heard it.

Mom and Marc and I were waiting at the hospital for hours this morning. Dad phoned Mom at 7 AM and said they'd already given him an injection and he was waiting to be wheeled into surgery.

Mom and Marc went to the hospital at 9 AM and I drove there about an hour later. Waiting was agony. Dr. Saltzman had told Mom that the surgery takes from 2½ to 5 hours, so when there was no word at 10:30, 11 AM, 11:30, we began to get very frightened that maybe something had gone wrong.

Mom was so upset but she maintained outward calm. I couldn't sit still and had to walk around the block several times. I called Evelyn at Kingsborough and told her to cancel my 12:40 class; she was very nice and said not to worry. I just hope I don't have to endure more waiting like that again.

When we left afternoon, they still hadn't brought dad into the recovery room. He'll be there till tonight, and I ordered a private nurse for the midnight-8 PM shift.

I went to Kingsborough for my 3 PM class. It went terribly, but it was a miracle I had the presence of mind to teach it. They didn't mark me as absent for the day, so that's all right. My office was changed to C-109.

Just when I called Jonny to tell him Dad's surgery was over, he reported getting a letter from the Police Department telling us that Marc's car had been found in a lot of wrecks right on E. 56th Street and Foster Avenue – the very place Marc told me was a haven for stolen cars when we passed it last night.

I've just spoken to Alice and Gary and Aunt Arlyne on the phone; Evie came in earlier; and of course Jonny called Aunt Sydelle and Grandpa Herb as soon as I gave him the word. Marc and Mom are at the hospital now, but we've had no news from them, and I'm not sure they're able to *see* Dad. I hope to go at 7 PM. Now we've just got to pray that no complications arise, either with the draining fluid or the facial nerve.

*

8 PM. I've just come back from Brookdale. I went there only to discover that Richie Lewis had been there and taken Mom home. Dad is going to be in

Recovery until 10:30 tonight. Mom wants to go back then and see Dad in his room, but I'm too exhausted to go; Marc will drive her.

I'm aware that Marc has borne the brunt of this so far, but he hasn't seemed to mind. He works with Dad every day and so is naturally closer with him. (Last night he told me that Dad had been impossible at work all week.)

Marc and Mom finally got to see Dad in Recovery after they had dinner; they were a little queasy at the sight of so many people just out of surgery, and they had to wear gowns.

Dad was very uncomfortable with a great deal of pain in his ear. (Downstairs, in the cafeteria, Mom had a similar pain in *her* ear. ESP?) He's bandaged all around his head and there are drainage tubes and IV tubes. He was coherent and talked about how he wanted to walk around.

Anyway, the important thing is that there was no malignancy and that they removed the tumor. I'm emotionally exhausted and I imagine Mom would be too, but for her desire to see Dad which, even if it's at midnight, seems to overcome whatever weariness she feels.

Jerry Klinkowitz wrote that he's quitting *Seems* and can't let anyone else bear the responsibility for publishing "Innovations"; he said Baumbach "hit the ceiling" when he read a copy of it. I suppose it's for the best – it won't be in print but Jon knows how I feel about him.

Tuesday, September 26, 1978

9PM. Tonight I went to see Dad at the hospital. His entire head is bandaged like a football helmet and he's carrying around a bag into which fluid and blood are draining. He's quite uncomfortable, with pains around his ear and cheek where they did the surgery. It's also hard for him to eat because he can't open his mouth wide enough to chew properly, and his throat is sore from the pipe that was there.

But for a man who had major surgery yesterday, he looks terrific. He's tired but he can sleep, and there's codeine for the pain. I went with Mom, and Irving and Doris Cohen were there, and so was Richie Lewis and his wife.

Dad had phoned at 8 PM last evening after they brought him back to his room; Mom and Marc went over and stayed until 11 PM. He was very restless because he couldn't get out of bed, but he was and is in remarkably good shape.

I think that this experience will actually benefit Dad. As he said to me and the Cohens in the day room,

"When a guy hands you a piece of paper and says this is what he's got to do to save your life, and you realize it isn't a dream, you see the rest of it is all shit. . ."

(Of course Doris remarked that when Ike Hoffeld thought he was dying in the casino in Vegas, he swore he'd never buy another Cadillac and his wife said she'd never wear her jewelry again. "But," Irving said, "Ike did buy a Continental afterwards and Ruth wore her jewelry – until she died of cancer.")

This afternoon Mom, Marc and Jonny were up there to see Dad, and so were Aunt Sydelle and her friend and Grandpa Herb and Grandma Ethel (whose doctor said her rash on her back has entirely cleared up, so the chemo is working).

Dad even called up Grandma Sylvia in Florida and told her about the surgery; she called him tonight and seemed reassured. The Littwaks also phoned from Miami tonight, and Lennie Schwartz from The Male Shop sent a plant.

Dad is so well-liked, his friends don't stop calling. I really have to admire the way he's held up through this. I've never thought of Dad as a strong person, but he is and I have increased respect for him.

He's bound to feel uncomfortable but as long as the tumor was benign and it's out, we can breathe easily. Maybe Dad's luck has begun to change and maybe he'll take a more relaxed view of things and be more positive – and *then* things will go his way more often.

Perhaps the surgery was a turning point in Dad's life. He finally stopped behaving as though things didn't exist; he faced up to this tumor instead of being an ostrich. I should take a leaf from Dad's book now.

Anyway, the family has been strong throughout this, and we've gotten a bit closer, I think. No matter what I may think or say, there's nothing better than a family – a good one, anyway.

Last night I spoke to Ronna and I could hear her mother screaming; Mrs. C had found out (from Ronna's sister) that Ronna had visited her father and was accusing her of being "a traitor to the cause." And it's not as if Ronna gets anything out of seeing Mr. C; he's usually very distant with her.

Ronna says it doesn't matter all that much anymore, but it must. She faces rejection from her father, and then rejection from her mother for undergoing the *first* rejection.

I stayed on a long time with Ronna even though I knew Wesley Strick from Taplinger was going to call.

"This is more important," I told Ronna, and it was. She said I helped her.

Wesley and I arranged a meeting at his apartment on the Upper East Side for next Monday evening – we'll see what happens. I'm fatalistic about my future now. I don't even care that they're beginning to observe the adjuncts at Kingsborough; if I don't get rehired, I don't.

A woman who's an editor of *Aspect*, Susan Lloyd McGarry, wrote that she'd like to do an essay on my work.

Wednesday, September 27, 1978

11 PM. I feel I can begin to relax a little. Tomorrow at 3 PM the woman from Counseling will speak to my students, so I have only one class on Friday to teach and then a four-day weekend. This past week has been a great strain on me, but at least I can sleep late tomorrow.

I took Mom to see Dad tonight. Marc and Donna also came, and Lou and Evie and Jerry and Jo also dropped by. Dad is very uncomfortable and hasn't slept since Monday, but he's getting along. Mom watched as they changed his bandage for another one this afternoon; they also took out the drain.

Dad seems almost a different person with his head wrapped in bandages and wearing pajamas, robe and slippers. He doesn't seem as excitable as he used to be; he appears more patient (is that where the term doctor's *patient* comes from?) and accepting. He complains but he endures.

There's a great strength within him, and I don't think he even knew he had it until he was tested like this. When I was very young, like all boys, I thought my father was invincible. More recently I've only looked at his weaknesses. Now I see a more balanced picture of him.

His beard gets scratchier every time I kiss him (and I kiss him hello and goodbye, even at the elevator with a crowd around).

Last night I dreamed of Dad and Grandpa Nat and other Jewish men in the Garment Center celebrating a holiday called Vexing Day, when they make clothes just for the sheer pleasure of it. All my life, the men in my family – Grandpa Nat, Dad, Marc, Uncle Marty, Grandpa Herb, Uncle Harry – have always been in the clothing business, and I've never thought about it much.

Monday, during that agonizing wait for some word to come out of surgery, Mom and I were looking through the *Metro* (one of the strike papers) and we saw an ad for a store advertising that it had famous brand jeans, including *Jim Dandy*. I wonder if Dad gets the same feeling when he sees someone wearing his pants as a writer does when s/he seems someone reading his/her book.

Dad's facial nerves are apparently undamaged, but he's depressed because he won't be able to lift heavy things or play tennis or run for 6-8 weeks (they don't want the scar to swell up). Dad will probably be home this weekend, so we can begin the Jewish New Year together.

I haven't written much about school this week. Maybe it's because it's basically a way I'm making money. My students are nice kids, but they're young and ignorant and don't know what they're doing in college – most of them, anyway. I get hoarse and try to teach and when each hour ends I can only think that I've earned another $22.

This morning I went to the Alumni Association office and picked up the Class Notes – God knows when I'm going to get a chance to do them, and the deadline is October 15. The next two weeks will be easy with only two 2-class days. But I've got the Class Notes and the meeting with Wesley Strick and next weekend is shot with George coming in for the Book Fair.

Back Bay View came out with my "Escape from the Planet of the Humans" – not impressive because it's already in *Disjointed Fictions*. Tom Whalen sent me *Lowlands Review* (a special issue, a great book of fictions by Crad Kilodney) and I got *Shenandoah, Rockbottom* and *Sun & Moon* in the mail. My "Clumsy Story" is advertised as appearing in their next issue. (It was accepted about 3 years ago.) I love getting little magazines, especially good ones. I also got *The People's Almanac 2* with my "Joanne Vincente" article – the book is a feast for a trivia freak like me.

Thursday, September 28, 1978

9 PM. Little relaxing was done today. This is the busiest I've been in years. I don't think I've had a free hour in the past 5 days. Even though I didn't teach today and just went in to hear my students' counselor talk with them, I couldn't relax.

Last night Bernhard Frank of *Buckle* called, wanting to know what happened to the piece on Susan Fromberg Schaeffer that I promised him. Spurred into action, I decided to stop stalling; it took half a dozen rewrites, but I finally came up with something that satisfied me.

What I like about Susan is her energy and independence and healthy self-confidence; she can be difficult and I can see why others call her arrogant, but I'm attracted to those qualities.

Josh called today, and in a funny way he got a job through me. Denis Woychuk went to LIU on the Friday when Dr. Tucker was stuck for someone to replace me; Denis got the job. So his tutoring position at NYCCC was open, as well as others, and Josh and Simon both went down for interviews and got the jobs.

Josh starts tomorrow; he'll be making $150 for 30 hour a week, which isn't great, but it's better than driving an oil truck. I feel a little funny about Denis taking my place at LIU; I can't imagine Margaret liking him as much as she liked me. But LIU is in my past now. Last spring I vowed that I would not come back in the fall, and surprisingly, I managed to keep that vow.

The mail brought *Small Press Review* and the *AWPress* (the new name for the newsletter of AWP – they listed *Disjointed Fictions* first in their "Books by Members"). Anyway, that gave me new places to submit to, and that took time. And money. God, with the 48-cent book rate, I've been spending over $20 a week on postage.

Anyway (that's the second "anyway" in two sentences: what's going on here, anyway?), there were a lot of chores to take care of today: drugstore, post office, gas station, copy center.

I spoke to Alice, who must be taking off for Reykjavik now. She's anxious to see her brother and to spend time alone in Paris, and getting away from work will be a relief.

Bob Wexler and Judy Frankel invited her to their wedding in Rhode Island, and she's decided to go. Bob bought a copy of *Disjointed Fictions* at the Eighth Street last week, so at least *some* copies are selling. I'm happy that he thinks enough of me to buy my work – it's pretty expensive for what's offered.

Bob's teaching history at Brooklyn, at Poly Tech, and in Manhattan at Baruch – what a grind that must be. Busy as I am, I can't imagine how I would have survived if I had a course at LIU.

My Kingsborough students are so obnoxious. Today, after class, Tyrone Hayward came up to me and asked, "Did you ever consider becoming a jockey?" I just gave him an icy stare. Look, I may not be a great and world-renowned writer but do I have put up with punks like that?

My students are all from the Disco Generation; they're so into themselves that they have no sense of society or history. None of them know what the Vietnam War was about, and to them, Robert Kennedy and Martin Luther King are vague historical figures.

Maybe Bill-Dade was more correct than I figured. God knows what these people will grow into – stylish

consumers, probably. Welcome back to the Silent
Generation of the 1950's. Jesus, it makes me glad I
was born when I was – when it was all right to be
different.

Dad looked good when Mom, Jonny and I went to see
him tonight. He'll probably be coming home on
Saturday. He walks the hospital corridors getting
involved with the doctors and nurses and patients
and says that hospital life – if you're not sick, as he is
not – can be relaxing. He's rather uncomfortable in
his bandages because he can't shave.

Friday, September 29, 1978

4 PM. For the last two hours I've allowed myself the
luxury of lying in bed and catching up on the soap
operas I now can watch only on Fridays. It's been
pleasant to feel bored after such a hectic week. One
class today; no mail to speak of; no errands to run.

I'm going to be observed a week from Thursday; Prof.
Rosalind Depas called me this morning to let me
know. I'll do the best I can. It's most likely a
formality anyway.

I woke up today to stunning news: Jonny calling up
from the kitchen to say that the Pope had died. I
turned on the TV and it was true: John Paul I, after

only a month in office, had died in his sleep. I feel worse than I did when Paul VI died, because John Paul was a more likable, *hamishe* man, if popes can have that Yiddish trait, and he never got to show what he could have done. I went back to sleep and had weird dreams about going to Mass. Pope Paul's death gave me nightmares, too.

I really don't know where my life is going, yet I feel I'm at the beginning of something new. I'll never feel about Kingsborough the way I felt about LIU – just as I never felt at home a student at Richmond as I did at Brooklyn College. Yet being at a new college is good for me more than just financially. If I can make it at Kingsborough – and so far I haven't proved myself to my satisfaction – I'll have learned that I can successfully adjusted to a new environment.

I haven't given much thought to moving out yet; my first paycheck is three weeks away. The term ends before Christmas and I won't be hired for the winter module, so if I teach in the spring, it won't start till the middle of March. If LIU offers me a course before that, I'll take it, though they may be pissed off at me by now.

I'm not even sure I want to remain in academia if academia means teaching remedial writing and reading. It's so wearying; I might be better off doing something which has nothing to do with literature and writing but which doesn't drain me so.

I'm 27 now and I'm becoming established as a short story writer; little by little, my strategy seems to have paid off. What I would like now is a job teaching creative writing, or fiction writing. (See, spare time makes me reflective – maybe that's bad.)

But if this week and this month of September have proved anything, it's that I'm not heading toward a rerun of my 1968 breakdown. No way – in fact, I haven't even given that a thought in weeks.

And now I've passed over the hump, the worst part of the tenth anniversary, and I am certain I am going to make it. John Paul I's death reminds me that life can be short and end unexpectedly. Bu at least he died a pope; I bet it was all worth it.

Of course Dad's operation tells me that we *can* recover, that it's not quite that easy to die. I do have hope now. I also feel more patient – especially more patient with myself.

I just spoke with Dad and he said the doctor took off the bandage today and if there's not any swelling, he can come home tomorrow. He's still in pain, of course. I'm not going to the hospital tonight. I don't think it's necessary and neither does Dad.

Ronna phoned last night. I suggested that she, Alison and I go to see *Interiors* at Kings Plaza. (I didn't tell her I'd seen it before because in the summer we made up to see it together.) At first I thought going out tonight would be too much for me, but I think it can only do me good.

It was 45° this morning when I awoke and summer seems a memory already. Aunt Sydelle's going to Florida to stay with Grandma Sylvia tomorrow. Arlyne and Marty took Grandma Ethel to the nutrition doctor.

Saturday, September 30, 1978

Midnight. I'm just coming off a writing high, having spent the last 4 hours finishing the final version of "Q & A," a 13-page story that is the best work I've done in a long time. About 24 hours ago I began it.

I felt like writing, but I didn't know how to get into it and then I remembered how the question-and-answer format worked so well for me in the pat. The writing flowed easily and I had a fairly good piece, but this evening I realized I could improve it if I wrote a second set of answers to the questions and set the answers side by side on a split page. It worked out very nicely and I feel relieved to know my creativity is not dead.

Dad's home now; Mom picked him up early this morning. He insisted on driving home (Mom said he's just like Grandpa Nat) but was tired afterwards and spent most of the day sleeping. When he eats, he's in a great deal of pain, as the chewing hurts the scar (which is very deep, but the doctors said eventually it will fill out).

I spent most of the early part of the day lying in bed; I couldn't awaken till 11 AM and then kept lying down. All the strain of the week had finally got to me. Sometimes you feel worse when a trauma is over; during the week my resources were drained, but the adrenalin and energy kept flowing. Now that the crisis is over, I feel a little overwhelmed, but certainly I feel much better than I did *last* Saturday.

I went to the village at 4 PM, stopped at the Eighth Street Bookshop, found my book in the window and four copies upstairs in the alphabetical fiction section. Laura (who wasn't there) took the book off display – the only copy sold was to Bob Wexler. I got some magazines and sniffed around; just getting into Manhattan for the first time in two weeks made me feel better.

Last evening was very pleasant. Mason came over here at 7 PM and I gave him my book and some ideas for lesson plans. Now he's calmed down a bit but he's still exhausted from dealing with those brats. I don't think I could hack teaching junior high; I'm having enough trouble with rowdy college students.

We drove over to Ronna's – I dislike the way Mason drives, so cautiously and meekly, but that's his style (mine is rush, cut in, and make that light) – and picked up Ronna and Alison. Alison and Mason met for the first time; they had being English majors in common. They're not a couple, nor did Ronna and I intend them to be, but I was surprised in Kings Plaza when Alison sat next to Mason rather than Ronna in the theater.

Interiors seemed better the second time; I recognize its many flaws, but it does raise serious issues, especially about creativity. Joey, the middle sister played by Marybeth Hurt, longs to be as creative as her interior decorator mother and her sisters, a poet and an actress. Joey has all their angst and sensitivity but no talent at all.

Sometimes I wonder just what I would do with all my problems if I weren't able to work them out in my writing. What does Ronna do with her frustrations? (She says she identified with Joey.) What do thousands of college-educated people who are unemployed and underemployed do?

After the movie the four of us went to the Floridian (rather than to a bar, a Mason had suggested; upstate he got into the habit of drinking a fifth of Jack Daniels every few nights), where we sat in a both next to Evie and Lou.

It was relaxing to get out; even if I couldn't be alone with Ronna, it's good to be her friend. Earlier in the day I spoke to Elihu, who's got an assistantship in the History Department and is teaching a 9 AM class – in his field, Early American History, for a change. He said his brother's not too crazy about Kingsborough and I can understand why.

Sunday, October 1, 1978

9 PM. October already – and the new Hebrew year 5739. The beginning of the Jewish New Year and the last three months of 1978. The other night Mason said, "Thank God for Rosh Hashona this year." Our family's observance of the holiday has changed to the point where, now, no one goes to synagogue, no one gets dressed up, and everyone but Jonny does everything (drives, watches TV, etc.)

I visited Grandma Ethel and Grandpa Herb this afternoon. Grandma Ethel told me her new diet is confusing to her: 7-grain whole wheat breads, bran, steamed vegetables, no sugar or salt, lots of nuts and fruit. I explained that it's basically a healthy and sensible diet low in fats, cholesterol, food additives and artificial ingredients designed to rid her body of toxins. "I may get healthy," she said, "but shopping in the health food store I'll go broke."

Psychology Today had an article on the nutrition revolution which has swept America. Certainly our refrigerator looks different than it did ten years ago. But then none of us exercised ten years ago, either. (This morning Dad walked a mile as Mom and Marc jogged.)

Speaking of ten years ago – I sat on their terrace with my grandparents and remembered that it was ten years ago, during my breakdown, that I stayed with them over the holiday while my room was being painted. I have photographs of all of us on that day: on one, I am skinny kid in sunglasses looking out towards the ocean.

Obviously I still look young – no one at Kingsborough believes I'm a teacher – but I can see lines around my mouth and eyes. (Too much sun, perhaps?)

Before I finally put my preoccupation with 1968 aside, I must say this: What troubles me about the experience of my breakdown is that after all these years, I cannot say definitely *why* I stopped functioning and I'm not quite sure how I "recovered" – started to function again.

Oh, I understand that various factors contributed to the breakdown: my mother's perfectionism and her own agoraphobia, my sexual confusion, fear of leaving childhood, even the political climate of 1968.

But to pinpoint the genesis of my illness, I cannot do. If I could travel back ten years in one of those time-barrier-crashing bubbles I used to see in comic books, I would love to interview the 17-year-old me and find out what I was feeling. I must have been feeling something besides fear, anxiety, humiliation and nausea.

Oh well – I spent most of this weekend reading, devouring everything in sight: all my little magazines, the newspapers (the three dailies are still on strike and their substitutes are poor), *The New Yorker, TV Guide, The People's Almanac 2*, essays from the texts I'm using, anything I could lay my hands on.

One of my students wrote in his self-profile that he "hates reading." How could that be possible? If something should happen and I couldn't write another word, at least I could read. I don't want to sound like a banal public service announcement, but reading makes life bearable in a way nothing else but other people can.

I wish I had unlimited resources and unlimited time so I could devour all the books I crave. TV is a pal and always there when you're lonely and bored, but books are trusted friends, people you save for important moments.

Maybe the National Endowment for the Arts should offer $10,000 fellowships to creative *readers* as well as to creative writers. Or they should subsidize those who buy books the way they do small presses that publish them.

Monday, October 2, 1978

5 PM. In a little while I'll be going to Manhattan to see Wesley Strick. I'll be missing our Rosh Hashona dinner with turkey and sweet potatoes, but last week I told Wesley that I'd come tonight.

I'm a bit ashamed that I did, that having a book published seems to mean more to me than dinner with my family. I'm not certain it does, and if I had more time to think about it, I might have asked Wesley to postpone our meeting.

I'm sure Rosh Hashona means nothing to him; he was probably brought up very assimilated. Now I suppose a non-observer like me sounds like a hypocrite saying that, but Rosh Hashona does mean something to me.

It is a time for reflection and renewal and asking forgiveness for my inadequacies and mistakes (I won't say *sins*). For me, this *is* the new year. And we have much to be grateful for. Last week Dad was in surgery and today he's walking around the neighborhood, enjoying the Yankees-Red Sox playoff game on TV.

My family and friends are all right, I'm all right, there's going to be peace talks between Egypt and Israel, the sun is shining, I'm on vacation – so what could be bad, no?

This morning I went to the Junction to xerox "Q & A" and some other things I'd written. At the corner of Flatbush and Nostrand, a young black woman said hello to me. I didn't recognize her and she said, "You're my English teacher." So I am.

The mail brought the first AWP Job Placement List with openings in colleges for next year. Now I feel more confident applying for jobs; after all I *am*, like the ads say, "a fiction writer with substantial publications."

I spent an hour writing cover letters and getting my resumés, bibliographies and writing samples together. I have to redo my resumé to add more publications, my teaching The Novel at LIU this summer, my job at Kingsborough, and perhaps the coming experience teaching creative writing in Harrisburg.

So I applied for jobs at Rutgers-New Brunswick, Rutgers-Camden, the University of Houston, the University of New Orleans, Virginia Polytechnic

Institute, the University of Cincinnati and the University of Arizona in Tucson.

What would happen if I got a job at one of those places? We'll see. But I do intend to apply for jobs everywhere, just as I submit everywhere. Eventually something will happen.

Sasha Newborn sent me a card asking why I haven't had a book published yet and inviting me to submit a long manuscript this winter. That's one reason that Taplinger is not something that will make or break me; eventually someone – Mudborn Press, Story Press, whoever – will publish a book-length collection.

I don't want my book to be an ill-conceived project or a premature one. I'm in a position where I don't have to beg from anyone. Honestly, I'm not all that desperate for Taplinger to do the book.

I suppose Mr. Strick and Wesley might think it strange that I'm not anxious. But this way *I'm* in control. It's not that I'm unsure of my talent –though I am; in some way, it's that I'm confident that eventually I'll be at least a minor-league talent.

Josh phoned last night. He and Simon start work at NYCCC on Wednesday. Josh said that they saw Laura at the movies on Eighth Street on Saturday.

I spoke to Ronna yesterday and she was attempting to get in touch with Sid and Carole. Today they're going to her grandmother's for dinner and tomorrow she and Susan intend to visit John at Rutgers.

I still haven't worked on the Class Notes; there doesn't seem time. What I need is a complete week off to catch up on all my reading, writing and other work. Things are happening for me, I feel it, but I'm still scared.

Of course I wouldn't be me if I weren't scared. Or maybe I'm scared *because* I think things are beginning to happen.

Tuesday, October 3, 1978

7 PM. Twenty-four hours ago I arrived at Wesley Strick's apartment. I had the beginnings of an anxiety attack on my way up to East 88th Street. When I got there, I found I had left his address in my other pants; also, my bladder was about to burst. I found his address after some difficulties by calling Information from a phone booth.

Wes Strick was what I expected, yet I was still impressed: lithe, very cool and stylish, dark and handsome in a casual, barely-formed way.

Although he's 24, I felt like an old man next to him, especially in my schlumpy $2.99 shirt, black pants and scuffed horrible shoes. He was wearing a denim shirt over a *Circus* T-shirt, white painter's pants and clogs.

But of course, if I were a sophisticated Manhattanite, I probably would not have been there. What makes my work interesting to Wes and his father and possibly to his others is that I'm an original, not stylish, and maybe a bit of a crank.

We sat for awhile getting to know each other – I told him I was nervous and the paranoid in me thought, absurdly, as I walked up the four flights to his place, "What if this is a trap?"

At first I thought Wes might be gay, but he just talks and moves in that East Side way. He's seeing a girl (he calls her a girl because he considers himself a boy) and seems *very* heterosexual.

He took me out to dinner (on Taplinger money) at a bar called Willie's, and on the way we stopped at one of those new Citibank stores and he used his card and punched buttons and money came out (a new rule in etiquette: one gentleman does not look at another's Citibank code number).

Fool that I am, I had Perrier water as Wes had a drink and chain-smoked. I told him how embarrassed I was to be talking about my work, and so for a while we talked of other things.

I told him about my life, the few things he couldn't piece together by reading all my stories, and he told me about his 100 acid trips in high school (now he doesn't even smoke grass), going to college at Vassar and Berkeley, his sister Ivy and *her* novel, the two *he* wrote (one is very long and is about Mozart), his work at *Rolling Stone*, how he feels about being the boss's son at Taplinger.

Finally he showed me the plan he has for the book: to bunch similar stories together, so that the repetition resonates off each other – stories about writing, women, famous people, "I" and the family. And he wanted to use "Raison d'Etre" as back jacket copy and "Notes on the Type" as, well, notes on the type. I sort of liked the idea.

When our waiter brought us the check, I looked him and asked if his name was John Ferro. He said yes, and I told him who I was and that we had gone to P.S. 203 together. It was nice seeing John; he hardly changed, said he was finishing up college.

Walking up Lexington, we came across a couple, and the woman hugged Wes. It was his mother and her longtime boyfriend, a famous Broadway set designer whose name was mentioned in this week's *New York*. Wes's mother had been away in the Hamptons all summer and it was the first time he'd seen her in months.

Back at his apartment, we went through the stories he'd chosen. He left out one or two of my favorites and put in a couple I think are weak, and we discussed changes he wanted made – almost all of which were examples of shrewd editing. This took about an hour, and it was fun; I wish I had Wes as an editor before.

It was 11:30 PM when we finished, and I said, "What happens next?" He said I should go over the stories and make changes and get back to him in a couple of weeks. I don't know if his father has given him a free hand or a green light on my book, but Wes did tell me that they think I could be "a cult figure." Ha!

Wednesday, October 4, 1978

9 PM. Reality time, boys and girls. What a miserable day. I got caught in the rain, got two traffic tickets, had a miserable time with my classes and generally felt lousy.

Last night I had nightmares about teaching at Kingsborough. I really hate my immature and obnoxious classes and I have as much difficulty controlling them a Mason does with his eighth-graders.

I arrived at school in a foul mood because some cop had to fill a quota and gave me (and God knows how many others) a ticket for making a left turn from a center lane – onto Shore Boulevard, where everyone does it. And since I couldn't find my insurance card, I now have to present that at the Motor Vehicles Department or another ticket will stand. Damn! Well, I'm going to plead not guilty and attempt to fight it. One of the little annoyances of life – shit.

My students are so babyish. Rosa Cordero, while walking with her friend, mentioned that she's pregnant. How come? her friend asked. "Oh, I think it was a mistake!" she giggled. *These* are people I'm supposed be teaching college-level subjects!

LIU was much better. If I put something on the board this term saying "Due Friday," they ask, "Is that for Friday?" And when I sarcastically say, "No, it's due Thursday," they believe me! They're devoid of ideas and common sense.

What a far cry from being on the East Side with Wes the other night. I now realize one of the reasons I enjoyed it was just to be with someone literate, intelligent and witty.

Yesterday I did the Class Notes – most of them, anyway, but today Marie Stein called and I'm sure she's got more for me to do. This weekend is the Book Fair, and I'll have no time to mark papers or prepare for being observed on Tuesday. I met Prof. Depas and told her the class is rough. I just feel so put upon. I can only feel grateful I had the presence of mind not to teach at LIU too.

There's no time for me to write. I would like to be revising my stories as Wes suggested, but I don't have time. I need help – in the form of a grant, an independent income, or whatever. Now I see there's no mystery why my productivity slackened in early August; since then I've spent too much time on teaching to be creative.

The period from June to July I was writing good things all the time, because I had the time. I *know* I could be really productive if I had more time to read and write and think. I am so frustrated. Monday night now seems like a visit to a world I never knew existed; of course, I've been aware of it all along, but recently I've spent so much time in banal, mindless company that I appreciate the Manhattan scene now.

I can't make fun of Alice and her crowd anymore; in a real way, I want to be a part of it. And damn it, yes, I am as attracted to the glitter of the literary would as much as Podhoretz said he was in *Making It*. I want an apartment of my own, like Wesley's or Alice's; I want a job where I can get respect and for which I'm well-compensated; I want to be with people I can talk intelligently to. I feel as though I'm drowning in idiocy.

The superficiality of Studio 54 may be absurd, but it's better than the idiots hanging around on street corners. I'm starving intellectually, getting nourishment only through books and magazines. That's one reason more graduate school might not be a bad idea.

Oh, I don't know. Sometimes – like on Monday night, when driving over the Manhattan Bridge, I thought of the phrase "a dream come true" – I think I'm going to make it, and other times I see myself going nowhere.

I've had absolutely no sexual desire for the past ten days. As the weather turns chilly and the days end early, I feel myself becoming a sterile container.

<u>Thursday, October 5, 1978</u>

1 PM. I need to write now because I don't have a therapist anymore. I feel very lost, very out of control. In an hour I have to go to Kingsborough. God, I hate facing my students. My car had to be taken in today. It's been missing and may need a tune-up; also, I may have an exhaust leak.

I went to the Alumni Association and picked up the rest of the Class Notes; I don't think I want to do them anymore. I'll have to take the rented car to school, though I'm not supposed to be driving it, and if I get stopped or into an accident, I'm in big trouble. Hell, I'm in big trouble anyway. I want to cry.

Last night's dreams were nice: I was capable of going everywhere. It was a blissful night. I fell asleep during *Network*. I haven't had an orgasm in about a week – I think that's a record. I have a tissue hanging out of my mouth now. My hair is too long. I have pimples. I feel fat. Crying: that's what I want to do. But I can't.

Oh, I hate being like this. I don't want to go to Kingsborough, I don't want George to come in for the Book Fair this weekend, I don't want to mark the 50 papers in my briefcase. I feel very much alone.

On Monday night when I got home from Wes's apartment, I called up Ronna and she was crying. She'd just gotten off the phone with Susan, who's planning her honeymoon with Marvin. All Alison talks about is marrying her boyfriend, and Ronna felt alone. I wish I could help her, but even if I wanted to marry her, she wouldn't agree to it. Or maybe she feels desperate enough to say yes.

I asked her if she was dating anyone; she isn't. She doesn't have enough time to see me or other friends.

I suggested that maybe she was crying about not getting married because that's something she can't control and thus easy to get upset about; perhaps what really was bothering her frustration about her career – something she can do something about.

In the end, Ronna thought I was right. We talked until 1 AM, and she said I helped her a lot. "I love you," I told her, and I heard her say, "I love you, too." If only love were enough!

Maybe it's just the weather – I don't know. I feel helpless, put-upon, pressed for time. My life seems at the mercy of 100 different things, none of which I can control. Unless – unless I am being like Ronna and using that as an excuse. (A good therapist might raise that point.) But, to tell you the truth, I don't want to explore myself now. I'd rather just feel rotten.

*

8 PM. Well, the car is fixed but now I've got a toothache caused by a filling that fell out. This isn't my day.

My class went as well as can be expected – Ivy Siegel seems to think the class is a dialogue between herself and me. The class's comments are usually fatuous, irrelevant or boring. They're such babies. I've just completed reading about 15 of their essays and I can't take any more. Some of them look as though they were written by sixth-graders.

I feel very angry at the whole situation. I don't think I want to teach at Kingsborough in the spring. I'm not sure I want to teach at LIU, either. Maybe I should try something else.

After all, I've had four years' experience by next spring; that should be enough to put me in a position to get a job teaching creative writing somewhere. I need a change. I'm not sure what it is I want to do, but teaching remedial writing isn't it. There's no joy in it anymore; it seems like a hopeless task.

Friday, October 6, 1978

7 PM. It's a lovely evening, mild and breezy. Last night was an incredible one; I slept for 12 hours, but I kept getting up. There was a furious thunderstorm going on, and at one point the thunder was so protracted I was sure I was hearing the Concorde take off or land.

I had a variety of magical dreams. I was sure I would remember them, but they're gone now. I spoke to Ronna last evening. She was feeling better; she's decided to make up her resumes and start sending them out.

This weekend Alison is moving into her own apartment; she has a way of manipulating Ronna, playing "poor little me," and making herself very dependent. In some ways I think Alison is a dead-ass. I like Susan better; now that Susan's with Marvin, she doesn't bug Ronna so much about not seeing her enough.

I've been complaining a great deal the past few days, I know, but I'm *not* desperately unhappy. What I am is dissatisfied. I can certainly tolerate teaching at Kingsborough another couple of months. The weeks will go by fast.

Toda, for example, wasn't that bad. Not that good, either, but I don't expect good things anymore. One of my office-mates tells me that she has a regular freshman class that's a dream, so maybe I've just lucked into a couple of rotten classes.

Perhaps part of it is I don't feel at home at Kingsborough. I have no friends there, as I did at LIU – but of course I didn't get friends at LIU till after a few terms of teaching there.

Nothing much happened today: I taught, I got three rejections, I went to the library (where I had a pleasant, literate conversation with a young librarian who just moved here from Syracuse and wanted to know where she could find a literary bookstore). I exercised, I watched TV (soap operas and the Yankee playoffs against Kansas City), I did *not* mark any papers.

And now I have a three-day weekend ahead of me. The Book Fair starts tomorrow and so does the *Assembling* exhibit at the Pratt Gallery. I tried to call George last night but couldn't get him in. I've had no word from him as to where he's staying, whether here or at his friend's house in Manhattan, and I don't know if he's driving in or coming by train. I might hear from him in a couple of hours.

I look forward to the Book Fair, of course, but there are some people I want to avoid: Jon Baumbach, Michael Largo of New Earth Books, a couple of others. And it's embarrassing to introduce yourself to people who've rejected your work. Every year the Book Fair turns into a bigger event, and this year, at Martin Luther King Jr. High School will probably get a lot of media attention. (The *Post* is back while the *Times* and *Daily News* are still on strike.)

Dad had his stitches removed today. The scars are not that unsightly, but it will take time for Dad's face to fill out – also, it's going to be a year before enough nerve ends grow so that the side of his face won't be numb anymore. But Dad's been working since Wednesday, and aside from twinges of pain, he seems fine.

Why is it that we can't remain grateful but always want more? Two weeks ago I would have given anything as long as my father's tumor was benign. Now, with the surgery successful, I am annoyed when I get a traffic ticket, enraged when my students act up, and depressed because of some little setback – or even the weather.

Candida Donadio, in a *New Times* article on the mysterious Thomas Pynchon, whose agent she is, said that no one can write a novel till they're 35 – that "today we have seen too much and been trampled too much and can't recollect the passions of youth until the tranquility of early middle age." Isaac Bashevis Singer won the Nobel Prize – a surprisingly good choice.

Saturday, October 7, 1978

10 PM. The Book Fair was today and I'm all book-faired out. Too many people, too many books, too much money I've spent. George called me from Manhattan, where he spent last night at his friend Stuart's place. Stuart used to work with him at the *Patriot-News* and now writes for *Soap Opera Digest*.

 I told George I'd meet him at Martin Luther King High, and I drove into the city right after breakfast, getting there just as most people were just setting up. This is the biggest Book Fair yet, but it's an out-of-the-

way place and didn't seem to draw much of a crowd.
I was helping Martin Tucker set up the *Confrontation*
booth; he doesn't seem annoyed with me at all. All of
a sudden George grabbed me from behind; God, it
was good to see him. He's working hard, hoping to
get into the editorial department (when I told him I'd
typed up a Class Notes item on the paper's editor,
Saul Kohler, BC '48, George told me to write Saul a
note about him).

Susan Lawton, George's printer and co-editor with
him of the *Tigris Journal*, soon arrived. She's a very
classy lady who lives with a fortyish artist in
Westchester.

Walking around or sitting at the table, the day was a
sea of faces. Some impressions:

Lynda Scott of *Gravitas* is a sick lady, sort of the
whore of the small press scene; she was cozy with
A.D. Winans, who doesn't look as crazy as I thought
he would. Len Fulton of Dustbooks looks like the
Marlboro Man, too eminent a figure for me to
approach.

Raymond Federman could Yves Montand with his
Gallic charm. Russell Banks, on the other hand,
seems standoffish; he's working on a nonfiction book
about Jamaica, he told me. Ed Hogan of *Aspect* is as
nice as I'd thought he'd be. His co-editor, Miriam

Sagan, is very funny – one of the sweetest people around.

Herb Leibowitz told me Tom Nevins is on his honeymoon; when I told Herb I didn't want to make a life of connecting comma splices, he said that's all he's doing this term. Peter Cherches of Zonepress is in the MFA program at Columbia now, hoping to get a job at BC or LIU.

Ken Bernard came to help Martin, and he brought his wife, children and father-in-law. Richard Meade of Story Press flew in alone; he seemed a bit lost with only one book to sell. I met Lee van der Velde, who accepted something of mine for *Helen Review*, I gave them a donation and got a free cookie.

Suzanne Zavrian said they've been getting a number of unsolicited intelligent reviews for her *American Book Review* and she thought that was a hopeful sign. Bob Hershon of Hanging Loose Press wore a John Greenleaf Whittier nametag, and his co-editor Ron Schreiber told me to submit some more things.

Rick Peabody from *Gargoyle* came down with a bunch of friends; he's broke and working as a stock boy. (He's a friend of White Ewe Press's Kevin Urick.) I avoided *Gallimaufry*'s Mary MacArthur, whom I once insulted in a letter.

Susan Lawton and I had lunch at a new expensive
Broadway place, The Saloon. When I ordered Perrier,
she said she'd *thought* I was an ex-alcoholic. Richard
Kostelanetz left early because his *Assembling
Assembling* show opened at a downtown art gallery.

I found a copy of *Junction* with "Guillaine-Barre
Syndrome" in it. Michael Lally autographed his book
for me and we talked about the heat and the crowd at
his Ear reading. I bought $25 worth of books and
magazines.

My feet hurt and my eyes hurt. I spoke for a long
time with David Gershator of the Downtown Poets'
Coop, who used to teach at BC's School of
Contemporary Studies; we talked of their crazy dean,
Carlos Russell, now Idi Amin's man in the U.S.

George is staying at Barbara Howard's house in Old
Westbury tonight. I dropped Susan off at Grand
Central and got home at 8 PM.

Sunday, October 8, 1978

9 PM. George never showed up at the Book Fair
today. I went there at noon and left with Ronna at
6 PM, mystified by his disappearance. OK, George
just called – he had gone through a real bummer of an
experience but it was his own fault.

I'd *told* him to call me if things didn't work out with Barbara Howard. Of course she never showed up. George waited till after 8 PM and got locked in the school. He kept calling the guy who knew Barbara but got no answer.

After being let out, George went to Penn Station, thinking maybe he would take the LIRR out to Old Westbury, but he was so disgusted, having sold one of my books and none of his magazines, that he decided to take the Metroliner to Philly. The only problem was that the next connection to Harrisburg wouldn't be for 13 hours!

He dialed his friends in Philadelphia but no one was home. Going into the men's room, he was followed by some black guy who poked through the bottom of George's stall. He spent the night lying on a bench like a bum, unable to asleep because he was afraid his admirer would bother him.

He caught a cold, of course, and when he got on the train to Harrisburg this afternoon, he discovered he'd gotten on a local going somewhere else; in his anxiety to leave, he hopped on an earlier train. They let him off at Ardmore, where he had to wait (outside – and today was very cold, with a high of 50°) another few hours until finally his train came.

He drove straight from the Harrisburg station to his parents' house, where he collapsed – and where he discovered his address book was missing. That book had all the addresses of his friends and *X* subscribers. Shit. The trip was a disaster for him. I feel terrible, but of course if he'd just called me from Penn Station, I'd have picked him up and he could have spent a comfortable night in this house.

I went to the Book Fair at noon, as I said, and waited and waited for him. Ed Hogan and Miriam Sagan went out to lunch, and I took care of the *Aspect* table for an hour. Then I went out to lunch by myself, and when I got back, Ronna arrived and kept me company and we walked around.

Michael Lally autographed his book for Ronna, and she thought he was licking his lips at the sight of me. Once I fantasized about sleeping with Michael, but I'm not really attracted to him.

Peter Cherches told me the Columbia MFA program is a joke, and Louis Pariscondola, who was taking care of the *Confrontation* table, said he's teaching English 10 this semester.

Edward Field signed a book for me, and Ronna was impressed, as she and Susan used to stay up late reading his work aloud. I met Geri Reilly (who was there with her twin Terri), who said she's still working for Social Security. She's pleased with her writing but hasn't been published yet.

Ron Sukenick and Steve Katz were walking around, but they've never been to friendly to me and are not likely to be now, so I didn't say anything to them. But I did meet Hal Jaffee, whose novel is being published with the Fiction Collective this spring.

I saw Michael Braziller of Persea Books and Les Von Losberg of *Junction* and the Poets' Union. Richard Meade of Story Press looked very alone (still), and Napoleon St. Cyr of *The Small Pond* looked strange wearing a paper hat.

Ed Hogan and I reminisced about the McGovern campaign; I feel like I've known Ed for ages. There are very nice people in the small press movement – it's crazy, but it's almost the way Student Government was in LaGuardia Hall was for me. In fact, it's exactly like it: the place where I fit in.

Ronna and I drove home and it was oh so good to hold her, talk quietly with her, kiss her. She's beautiful. Today I first saw her from a distance, and what registered immediately was that she was a beautiful woman, not the fact that she was Ronna.

Monday, October 9, 1978

7 PM. Columbus Day makes me feel very nostalgic. Especially today because it was so cold: 40° when I

awoke this morning. I took a walk late this afternoon, and I *never* take walks. But it's fall and somehow it seemed necessary.

I remember other autumns. 1968: breaking down, unable to sleep, doing nothing, going nowhere but group therapy. 1969: being a freshman, the Vietnam moratorium, going to classes after eating lunch (a cheese sandwich, soda, an apple and Sara Lee marble pound cake) and watching *Where the Heart Is*. 1970: being active in student government, meeting most of the people who would be important to me. 1971: breaking up with Shelli, crying uncontrollably, cutting my hair, getting into herbs, wearing flannel shirts.

1972: dating Ronna, bringing her flowers and sage rinse for her hair, taking her to see *Jules and Jim* which she thought very weird, fogging up the windows of my Pontiac. 1973: driving out to Staten Island at twilight for classes, seeing Ronna still, still hanging out in LaGuardia Hall. 1974: working at Alexander's and hating it, being in the MFA program and loving it, dinner at the Pub with Simon, breaking up with Ronna, it being bad but not terrible but still bad enough to hurt, ending therapy.

1975: teaching at LIU Tuesday and Thursday mornings, getting my first stories accepted, worrying about the future. 1976: hoping Carter would win, teaching and not being a student for the first

September in 20 years, being lonely and answering ads in the *Village Voice*, stories beginning to come out. 1977: again at LIU, still writing, stories coming out all over the place, frustrated at home, missing Ronna and Avis and Grandpa Nat.

1978: here we are. I held Ronna last night. People recognize my name. I might have a book published. I miss being an undergraduate, having loads of friends and time to hang out. I'm scared about being observed teaching tomorrow, but I think that's only because I feel I *should* be scared. I dread the early darkness, the end of summer and sexiness, I dread the cold.

But this term will end in two months and I am really looking forward to December and January. I want to relax, to write, to see Avis when she comes in, maybe finally get to Florida to see my grandparents. But I have ten weeks to get through before that.

I don't enjoy teaching at Kingsborough and I'm not certain I want to remain a teacher. I find it hard to write as much or as well as I used to. My teeth hurt often. I look good these days; it's a year since I got my lenses. I feel depressed now but the problem isn't really situational, it's just *life*, and I guess it's not really a problem at all.

Today I xeroxed my stories and marked papers and prepared for tomorrow's lesson and listened to soap operas and got bored. Dad worked a full day today, two weeks (they went so fast) after his surgery. Jonny passed his road test and has been taking out the Cadillac every night.

Alice sent a postcard from Spain. Tom Whalen accepted "The Greatest Short Story That Absolutely Ever Was" for *Lowlands Review*, calling it "the ultimate Grayson." *Tailings* came out with my meditation, "Conjectures." The chairman of the English Department at Rutgers-Camden wrote he was impressed with my vita.

I feel sleepy but there are more papers to mark. It's only 7 PM and I don't have to get up early anymore. And after working tomorrow, it will be Wednesday – Yom Kippur – on Wednesday. Yom Kippur, a holiday/holy day.

Tuesday, October 10, 1978

8 PM. It's Yom Kippur and I feel quite relieved. My observation went better than I could have expected. I spent hours preparing the lesson, I wore a sport jacket, I was "up" and loose, and the class, God love them, really came through for me; they must like me after all. Prof. Depas showed me her form after it was filled out and she checked all the "good" and

"excellent" boxes and had no adverse criticism. In
fact, she asked me how long I had been teaching.

I felt jubilant afterwards and had a hamburger in the
cafeteria overlooking the beach. Suddenly
Kingsborough seemed a delightful place, and I was
filled with affection for the school and for my
students.

Today was a kind of turning point. For the next two
months, I won't have to worry about being observed;
I can get down to business. Even my 3 PM class went
well; I let them out early for the holiday. I handed
back papers today, and though the marks were low,
nobody complained to my face.

I spoke with Stephen Sponk and Steve Antelli, and
both of them expressed the same frustrations I've
been having with my classes. So I'm not alone, and
not getting through to the students isn't my fault. I
feel 100% better about teaching at Kingsborough.

The rest of the week is easy, and I've just got to keep
on trucking until the end of the semester. Friday is
finally payday, and I think that will ease my
sufferings considerably. I feel good about myself
again – as a teacher, anyway. As for myself as a
writer, well. . . Avis wrote that she didn't like most of
Disjointed Fictions: "too much I, I, I," she said. I've got
to cut out all this super-self-conscious stuff; Avis is a
fairly representative person.

Last night I came across a notebook detailing things that happened in the summer of 1972. It was fantastically interesting, but I have no idea how to present it in fiction. There are too many characters to make a coherent story, and I'm sick of incoherent stories.

I got three rejections today, plus the invitation to participate in *A Critical Assembling*. Kostelanetz and Korn got an NEA grant (the panel probably figured it would shut Richard up) to do an *Assembling* where they would print the camera-ready material – it's all supposed to be on criticism of avant-garde or experimental literature.

Among those invited along with me are Ed Hogan, Ron Sukenick, George Economou, Clarence Major, Dick Higgins, and some really heavy hitters: Susan Sontag, Allen Ginsberg, Ihab Hassan, Northrop Frye, Marshall McLuhan. I'm very flattered to be in such company and I look forward to the challenge of writing something that's not fiction.

I've discovered since I did the piece on Susan Fromberg Schaeffer that I enjoy doing assignments and that I enjoy the intellectual challenge of rewriting a dozen times.

Avis told me all about her French vacation in her letter, and I got a card from Teresa, who went to

London with her roommate Mary. Ronna phoned me this afternoon and asked if I could come over and help her make up her resumé, so I'll leave in a few minutes.

Last night I typed up a new dossier to include my job at Kingsborough and new publications; I've got to send it off to Rutgers-Camden. I feel that my getting somewhere is inevitable; sooner or later, I'll have a writer-in-residence job or a publishing job or something. Working is not so bad. If I hadn't worked today, I wouldn't feel this glorious sense of accomplishment and also the relief at *not* having to work tomorrow.

Wednesday, October 11, 1978

7 PM as Yom Kippur ends. It was a glorious day to believe in Brooklyn. Giovanni da Verrazano wrote in his journal of "this pleasant place situated among certain little hills, from amidst which there runs down to the sea an exceeding great stream."

I feel very boroughistic this evening after reading this new magazine *Brooklyn*. There was an article by Rob Edelman on all the movies about Brooklyn, from King Vidor's *The Crowd* to *Saturday Night Fever* and the forthcoming *Boardwalk*.

Also, there was an article about the NBC studio on Avenue M, where they film my favorite soap opera, *Another World*. When the building was a Vitagraph film studio, Rudolph Valentino worked there as an extra for a day and Leon Trotsky made $7 a day there as a set designer. And in 1954, NBC filmed two series there: Gene Lockhart as *His Honor Homer Bell* – they used Midwood High School as the exterior of Judge Bell's courthouse and LaGuardia Hall as the town hall. There should be a story or poem in all of this.

Last evening Alice phoned. She came back from Europe two days early and had tried to return earlier but got stranded for two days in Luxembourg, where there was nothing to do but see junk movies like *Coma* and *The Swarm*. The best part of the trip was her visit with her brother, who took her all over Iceland. Paris was not as exciting as it had been for Alice; she didn't meet anyone except "a lot of creepy Arabs crawling around."

Tonight Alice left for Miami Beach, where she'll be covering a conference on teenage unemployment sponsored by Burger King. Avis has never been to Miami before and I was in the rare position of telling Avis the lowdown on a new city. She's even staying at the Carillon.

That reminds me: I definitely want to go to Florida this winter. I'll have the time off, and I haven't seen my grandparents in years. If I want to fly down there in January, I'd better make reservations soon.

Last night, after dinner, I went to Ronna's to help her with her résumé. She's finally getting her act together and will look for work at newspapers in the Northeast. Alison was just leaving as I arrived, and Barbara was prancing around.

Ronna and I worked on the résumé and we talked about her dinner with Sid and Carole the previous night, when Susan also tagged along. They looked terrific, Ronna said, and are both doing very well. I suppose I shouldn't be envious of Carole, who hasn't published any of her fiction yet, but she did get two $1000 grants out in Indiana.

Ronna and I sat on the living room couch and held each other and kissed. Writing this sounds so banal. For the first time in years, she said "I love you" to me without my saying it first. We made out like crazy for hours, but I didn't think it was cool to have sex in the living room with other people in the house, so I left at 1 AM.

"We both know what we're going to do when we get into bed," Ronna said. I don't know about her, but I had an incredible orgasm; I never felt the semen spurt out with such force. I felt absolutely wonderful and fell asleep and had a dream about space travel in

which I was dizzyingly flying out past Saturn and
Uranus. It was very eerie.

Today I woke up late but took care of a lot of errands.
I got my insurance card ticket dismissed, took a
haircut, xeroxed my dossier, went to the bank, and on
the way I managed to take a ride through Prospect
Park and enjoy the Indian summer weather.

Thursday, October 12, 1978

6 PM. I've been feeling very irritable today. Little
things have been getting on my nerves – such as all
my pens running dry as this one is doing. I'm very
dissatisfied with myself. I've gotten fat again. I
haven't done any work on editing my stories for Wes.
Mrs. Ehrlich wrote me a note suggesting I would
really like to come back to therapy, and that made me
angry, partly because it's true.

I've been spending too much money lately – money I
don't have. I have only about $300 in the bank, and
my check next week will be eaten up quickly. I don't
know if I can afford an apartment.

I'm annoyed at Avis for saying I write too much
about myself. I'm annoyed with an editor for
rejecting my story and saying "this is very poorly

organized." I'm annoyed – as usual – with my babyish students. Most of all, I'm annoyed at myself.

I don't know what I want, and I seem to spend most of my life on trivia. Nothing important ever seems to get done; only insignificant tasks get accomplished. I finished the Class Notes and gave them to Marie this morning. I hope I don't have to do another one.

Mom uses my car to pick up Jonny from school and it's always a close call making it to my 12:40 class. My parents don't understand my frustration about not having time to write.

They'll never understand my gayness; I talked in broad terms about homosexuality over dinner and they're so dense about it. At 27, I'm at the point where I'm tired of trying to pretend I don't feel things that I do feel.

Yesterday I got a letter from Bobby Mahoney, whose *Voice* ad I answered a couple of weeks back. Bobby is 25; I had to go to the library to remember his ad. It turns out he's "straight," but is interested in "trying something new."

I called him this afternoon and he seemed very nervous, as if I was about to rape him over the telephone. He works at Random House as an editorial assistant and Wants To Write; I don't think he actually *does* write.

But I shouldn't be so sarcastic. Anyway, I tried to arrange a meeting with him (he asked for something "very casual – over coffee or a drink"), but he said this week was no good and he'll get back to me next week.

He sounds like a nice guy, but I won't ever hear from him; he's too scared. Damn it, I'm not scared anymore – not of being myself and not of telling the truth.

Do you know how hard it is to convince 17-year-olds that clichés are bad? For years they've heard nothing but clichés and now they look on an original phrase – or an original thought – as something to avoid like the plaque (dental plaque, that is). Maybe I'll read some Edward Field or Michael Lally poetry as an antidote.

I suppose I'm too hard on my students. They've young, not sure of themselves, and it's risky for them to be themselves. I'm not so young anymore; I may not know what I'm doing, but I know who I am and don't have time to make excuses.

I was at the gas station filling up when Nestor, Marc's friend who used to be a creepy drug addict, came over and told me how much he enjoyed "Bartleby the Scrivener," which he'd just read. We talked about it – I told him I'd taught it this past summer – and I began to like Nestor for the first time.

People can and do change. Carl Rogers thinks we ultimately progress, and I'd like to believe that. Maybe I'm angry because I know what I'd like to do (edit my book, return to therapy, get my own apartment, be more adventurous sexually) and am not doing it. It looks as though I'm refusing to take responsibility.

Friday, October 13, 1978

4 PM. It's a lovely, bright afternoon. The weekend is upon me, and this is always the best part of the weekend: the anticipation of it. I hope – no, I am determined – to begin editing the book for Wes this weekend. Tonight I'm seeing Ronna but I have no plans for Saturday and Sunday, and I don't have much schoolwork to do.

Five weeks at Kingsborough have gone by, and I'm starting to feel at home there. I've begun to like my students and even managed to have a good time in class today. They may be stupid but they're nice; I haven't given them much of a break.

Today I got a letter from the Acting Chairman of the English Department at the University of New Orleans. He acknowledged my application, saying my "credentials" are "very impressive." His response (in the AWP Placement List he said he'd only respond "if there is a possibility of appointment") and the one from Camden-Rutgers make me feel as though I have made progress from the days when I got form letters.

Evidently I'll be considered seriously for jobs now. This New Orleans professor said he wants to interview me at the MLA Convention in late December (it will be in the city this year, so that's convenient).

Last night on public TV, they were showing the documentary *Word Is Out*, interviews with 25 gay men and women of all types. Peter Adair, one of the filmmakers, was the friend of Skip's who came to Brooklyn College several years ago. He showed two films, about Vietnam and a San Francisco gay pride parade. Afterwards I went out to lunch at The Pub with him, Skip, Mason and Libby, Vito and Dom. I remember it as a very pleasant time.

If I do go to see Mrs. E – and I may – one of the things I will tell her is that I've come to accept my gayness as something natural, a part of me. It does take a long time. I see that guys like Bill-Dale and Bobby Mahoney haven't yet accepted themselves sexually, so I feel ahead of them.

After the film, I watched an episode of *Family* where a young couple decide not to remarry because, while they love each other, they cannot make a go out of it as a husband and wife. It made me cry. I love Ronna,

I care so much for her – too much to attempt to hold onto her.

If that's true, why am I seeing her tonight? Because I want to, I guess, and because it's her half-birthday. Six years ago, on another Friday the 13th, before we were going together, I sent her a birthday card ripped in half. I want to do the same tonight.

But maybe I'm not being fair to her. She knows all about my proclivities (I love that that word is never used except when referring to homosexuality) and says it doesn't matter. Still, my continuing to see her may be bad for her.

I love Ronna more than I could love any woman, but I think I could love a man more deeply; anyway, I'd like to try to find out. It would be nice if Bobby called.

I care for Ronna a lot more than I care for our relationship – she's my friend – and I would prefer her not seeing me to her being hurt by me. I feel as though I'm taking and taking from her and not giving enough in return.

I suppose it's not my responsibility to worry about Ronna not getting enough out of our relationship. She 'd tell me, wouldn't she, if she was dissatisfied? Mostly we're friends.

This morning in the shower I decided that I'm not at all worried about growing old. Sometimes I think the nicest time of life is just after 50 when, like Dad or Edward Field, you've passed your mid-life crisis and at last feel comfortable with yourself.

Saturday, October 14, 1978

8 PM. Any day when your muffler falls out of your car in Chinatown isn't exactly a great day. I went into Manhattan to see the *Assembling Assembling* exhibit at the Pratt Graphics Center – it wasn't anything much, and my contribution looked stupid.

I was driving back to Brooklyn on the FDR Drive when I decided I would exit at South Street and get the Manhattan Bridge. (It was the first time I'd ever done that, and superstitious me won't do it again.) I started hearing a noise when I accelerated, and then – *clunk* – on Division Street my muffler dropped, bending the rear out of shape as I dragged it.

I took it to a gas station where they cut it off and I drove home via Flatbush Avenue very noisily. Monday I'll bring it in to Bob. It needs a whole new system and will probably cost a fortune. My car is falling apart; I don't know how much longer I can keep it patched together.

Getting to Kingsborough by public transportation will be a pain in the ass – and with Dad and Marc gone, there'll be no car for Mom, either (nor Jonny).

Today was my Friday the 13th, but I'm trying not to let it get to me. I didn't get to edit my manuscript today, nor do I think I can do it tonight. Is it a kind of writer's block? Am I deliberately avoiding getting my book together? Because I'm afraid of success? Because I resent Wes's suggestions?

Last evening Ronna and I went to see a late movie at Kings Plaza. Beforehand we talked about her career and how she's got to get her shit together; so far, she's just been playing at *wanting* to be a reporter and doing nothing about it.

I told her she's not informed enough; she doesn't know half the things I know about what's going on in the press. She says I've helped her more than anyone through this rough period for her.

Ronna doesn't see Susan much because of Marvin, and she resents Alison's constant presence. Alison was watching the World Series with Mrs. C and Billy when I arrived. Ronna's mother can't stand Alison's nasal whining, but Alison doesn't know that. She's your basic fuck-up; gave out the wrong address, for example, to her mother, boyfriend and the movers bringing a couch. In this respect, she makes Ronna look like a Miss Preparedness.

After the film (*Who Is Killing the Great Chefs of Europe?* – mildly amusing), Ronna and I came back to my basement, where I told her what I was feeling about our relationship. She said she was satisfied with the way it is going and doesn't expect anything more; if she does want something deeper – or different, anyway – she'll look elsewhere.

We made love and it was very pleasant, warm and tender, if not particularly passionate. Ronna got more out of it than I did, although I'm not complaining. It's very nice to hug and kiss and lick and hold and lie next to Ronna, and I would love to be able to spend the night with her. I like her ass, her breasts, and I'd say I liked her cunt if I could bring myself to use that word.

As I wrote yesterday, Ronna is everything I'd want in a woman – beautiful, caring, intelligent, independent, funny – but she isn't a guy. And if I think a man will be better, or at least different – then, as Ronna told me, it's my responsibility to find one.

It was very nostalgic to be in my basement with Ronna till 2:30 AM, and to drive her home at that wonderfully alive dead hour. I gave her a ripped half-birthday card, similar to the one I gave her six years ago, on another Friday, October 13th. We are good and old friends who share a great deal. But I am not the man for Ronna, and Ronna is not the man for me.

She went to New Jersey this weekend, to spend a day with Phil at Princeton and then to visit John at Rutgers.

Wendy called today, asking for my English-teacherly help on an essay she's writing for her application to the Wharton business school at the University of Pennsylvania. It must be nice to be 17 and applying to colleges.

Sunday, October 15, 1978

4 PM. I'm feeling somewhat better today. Last evening I began to edit the stories for Wes. It went more quickly and more painlessly than I had expected. I even *wrote* a bit last night: just a fragment, nothing complete.

But anyway, I feel I've caught up on things. I've prepared my classes for the coming week, and for the 11 class I've begun an outline of the rest of the term's work. I marked all the papers that needed marking. The Class Notes are finished, so I don't have to worry about them, and I'm not going to expend energy, time and postage on sending out stories to magazines.

The book is more important now, and so is following up on job prospects. I've already laid the groundwork for my getting somewhere. It won't be a meteoric rise out of nowhere (God, what clichés! I'd better pay attention to my own lectures), but it's better to play the tortoise, I think.

After all, I don't expect to begin writing a solid novel until I'm 35 or so. (That seems to be the norm for novelists today, and with my generation's extended adolescence, it may become even older in the future.)

This morning I saw on TV a woman of 55 who'd just published her first novel after short stories since college. I want to become more relaxed about "getting ahead," less manic, more thoughtful. I can feel myself becoming more comfortable with who I am.

I don't have the need to write egomaniacal stories (like those in *Disjointed Fictions* which Avis objects to). I haven't written much in the past three months, not because of writer's block, but because I haven't had the time and because I'm working out a new way of dealing with my fiction.

I'm not certain what will happen to my writing once this transition period is over, but it's got to be something new. I could be turning out more stories based on my own "formulas," but why bother? I've given up writing for writing's sake.

I've been speaking to several of my friends. Josh is finding that he knows more about grammar than he thought he did as he tutors at NYCCC. He and Simon both tutor 30 hours a week and the pay isn't great, but Josh prefers it to driving an oil truck. Most of the students are black, and Josh tries to get the few white female students for himself.

Last night I called Mikey, who's still getting off for Jewish holidays at Cardozo. Under his internship program, Mikey defended his first client in Bronx Criminal Court; he plea-bargained and got the guy three months.

Alice phoned a little while ago. The rooms and the food at the Carillon were to her liking, and she had an affair with her first black man, a wealthy Oklahoman, 30, who's been married four times.

The conference was pretty boring and it will be a miracle if she can get a story out of it. Alice has decided to stay at *Seventeen* for another few months before she begins actively job-hunting again.

I discussed my own career plans with her. She thinks I'm crazy to apply for jobs outside New York, and to be truthful, I'm not sure I want to be in New Orleans or Tucson or Houston for a year. The job would have to be a very good one – I wouldn't want to teach just comp courses – and the money would have to be good.

Tomorrow I'll have to take two buses to
Kingsborough, but I'll survive. Mom and Dad are at
a birthday party for the Cohens' grandson Jordan,
Marc is at Donna's, and Jonny is lifting weights in the
basement. I've been inside all day and I'm not going
out now. I slept twelve hours last night; it was
wonderful.

Monday, October 16, 1978

7 PM. Last evening I watched the Yankees clobber
the Dodgers. They now need one game to win the
Series. I had some trouble falling asleep and didn't
get up until 9:30 this morning.

Dad took my car into Bob's station earlier, so I had to
call car service to get to school. (I decided a taxi
would be worth it.) Before leaving, I finished the
minor editing on my stories for the collection. Now
I've just got to completely rewrite a few stories --
"Uncle Irving," "Go Not to Lethe," "The Mother in
My Bedroom."

I taught my 12:40 class fairly well, going over simple
and compound subjects. Rosa Cordero is getting a bit
too friendly with me. I think she misunderstood my
interest in her classwork as something personal. She
told me she talks about me to her mother all the time,

and started to tell me something, then said, "I'd better not. . . It's too personal."

God, she may be in love with me! What a revolting thought: to be loved by a near-moron. I'd better be more distant with her; all I wanted was to stop her from disrupting the class. A month ago she used to burst into laughter at the sight of me.

I worked out a schedule for the 11 class, and I've pretty much got the rest of the term under control. There were notices in our mailboxes about final exams, so you know the term's beginning to end – at least psychologically. Our adjunct payroll is this Friday, November 17, and January 5. I still don't know how much my checks will be.

After a lesson paragraph development, I grabbed a taxi home and got here by 4:15 PM. The new pope, John Paul II, is the first non-Italian in 450 years; he's a relatively young Polish cardinal who appears to be intelligent and firm.

I don't know why I've been so fascinated by the conclaves of cardinals this year. The mystery and the rituals involved in the election of a pope are something Judaism is lacking. And of course I love all kinds of elections and always have.

Without the papers, it's been hard to follow the off-year elections for Congress and the governorships,

but I've been trying. I think Gov. Carey will now
squeak past Perry Duryea next month.

You know what's beginning to scare me? I think I'm
writing like my students. Recently these diary entries
have become boring, banal, and awkwardly
composed. I need a dose of good writing, of
something really sharp, where every word is the right
word.

The weather's changed again, to very cool. I'm
expecting to catch a cold any day now. I've had no
mail for two mail deliveries, and I'm beginning to feel
very isolated, as if I'm just drifting.

Late last night I was thinking about my diaries.
Maybe I should end the practice of recording my
thoughts every day – perhaps it's come to the point
where it detracts from my "creative," "public"
writing. I would like to go on to August 1, 1979, and
finish out a decade.

Isn't it an accomplishment to have recorded a whole
decade – the Seventies – in these weird red books? It'
definitely been an influence on the way I write, and
on the way I view the world.

Giving equal space to each day make me feel that
there are no real turning points, that both bad times
and good times pass, that life is to be lived in day-

tight compartments (I remember that phrase from Dale Carnegie, whom I read in high school).

I look on my life – and the lives of my family and friends, and on *history* – as a kind of adventure, a blank page to be filled in at a later date. I'm not that scared of life anymore; like a soap opera, it always seems to continue, no matter what.

Tuesday, October 17, 1978

5 PM on a bright, chilly afternoon. You can just *feel* winter lurking ahead.

I've discovered how to add hours to the day: turn off the TV. It's incredible how I used to waste evening after evening plunked down in front of the tube. Maybe one of the reasons I felt so good at Bread Loaf was because there was no TV there.

I hate being a TV addict, filling up my mind with air. In our house, the first thing we do in the morning is to turn on the TV and at night the last thing we do is turn it off. Most people in America live like that, I would imagine. When my students described their rooms, each of them mentioned their TV set – a couple said it was the most important object in the room.

Last night I read Michael Lally's books; I think he's super, although sometimes I don't "get" his poems. I have a sensibility similar to his, especially when it comes to sexuality. He is a gay man who falls in love with women as well as boys – that's how I see myself, too. The letter was kind of a come-on; I wrote that I used to have a crush on him but now that I'm mature, I just respect him. I think I would like to have a relationship with him. I enclosed "Go Not to Lethe" and of course I hope he'll be so charmed he will want to meet me.

Two encouraging rejections came in today's mail – that's better than nothing. I called Wes Strick at his apartment, purposely getting his answering machine (he has a tape on which he talks like a hood trying to sell his record collection, as on TV) so that it's now his turn to call me. I'm very embarrassed about this book project; I still half-believe that they're putting me on.

My classes went well today, though I'm a bit hoarse. I got back, and had to sign my observation report; I couldn't have asked for a better one.

Grandma Ethel and Grandpa Herb stopped by this morning on their way home from NYU Hospital. According to her doctor, Grandma Ethel is making excellent progress and the cancer is retreating or whatever the proper word is.

The new health-food diet she's on is making her crazy. She doesn't understand why she's eating all these strange foods, and sometimes makes horrendous mistakes; for example, her doctor told her to drink fruit juices, so she bought Hi-C and Hawaiian Punch – which are nothing but sugar, water and Red Dye #2.

Taking 31 vitamin and mineral tablets a day is too much for her to handle, and she doesn't know how to prepare foods organically. At 68, she's changing a lifetime's eating habits and it isn't easy. Grandpa Herb, from whom Mom gets her compulsiveness, doesn't like the change in his lifestyle, either.

Last night I called Vito at the newsstand. He feels he isn't going to get anywhere as an actor; I don't know if he tries hard enough, but I'm sure it's an even tougher field to break into than writing. "If my biggest news is that I've got cable TV," Vito told me, "my life can't be going too well."

Seven years ago today was the day Shelli and I broke up, the last day I slept with her, the day I learned she was having an affair with Jerry. The same chill is in the air today, I feel the same dry throat, my hands feel a similar roughness. I dislike this in-between weather: 45° is too cool to be comfortable outside and not cold enough to make me feel energetic.

Wednesday, October 18, 1978

7 PM. It's night out already. In another two weeks Daylight Savings Time will end and it will start to get dark at 5 PM or so. We're heading into winter. I feel tired after teaching two classes a day for three days straight.

While I now have the respect of my students and the behavior problems are minimal, I still feel enervated after teaching without a day of rest to keep me going. But I'm doing this for the money, plain and simple. I have to constantly remind myself that the term will end in mid-December and I'll have two months free.

My classes are in the middle of the day, and while I'm spared having to get up early, there's not enough time in the morning to get any real writing done. And when I get home, there's only an hour before dinner, and after that I'm tired. Of course tomorrow I don't have to be at Kingsborough until 3 PM.

Wes phoned me back last night and we agreed to meet Saturday afternoon to discuss things further. I won't permit myself to believe that Taplinger is actually going to publish the book; I'm sure Louis Strick would rather hold off until something more substantial comes along. But I like Wes, and the whole thing is an interesting experience. Eventually somebody will publish my book; I have faith in myself.

This morning two copies of the spring (!) issue of *Texas Quarterly* arrived. It's a large, beautifully-bound magazine, rather stuffy and intellectual, but this credit will do me good in academia. Certainly "I, Eliza Custis" is nothing like *Disjointed Fictions*; it's the opposite of experimental, and Kostelanetz, Klinkowitz, and Baumbach would all hate it.

But I read it during my break today, and I think it's good in one respect: I've managed to create (of course I had the help of some material – or did I plagiarize?) a character totally different from myself, a character one *cares* about, not a trick, not an illusion.

By the way, Klinkowitz wrote me that his design editor, Roy Behrens, sent the original of "Innovations" to Baumbach. Now Jon has the only copy, and I'm sure he won't return it. The only other copy I had I sent to Ed Hogan at *Aspect*, and if I don't get that back, the story has been lost. The Lord works in mysterious ways; maybe it just wasn't meant to be.

I spoke to Ronna last night and we made plans for Friday evening. She had a marvelous weekend in New Jersey. She and Phil visited various friends in Princeton, and on Sunday she, Susan and John had a chicken dinner, during the course of which Ronna told John she was in love with him and he asked her if I would consider sleeping with him. (I told her to tell him I might.)

During the night I had this dream: Avis – or maybe Ronna – had to do a report on homosexuality. Scott drove us around on a Sunday night following a party and we found that the Mill Basin branch of the public library had its lights on.

It wasn't open, but Cassie Levinsky (Scott's old girlfriend) and her husband were using the library as their home and they let us in. We reminisced about our college days, Cassie asked me if I was a writer, and Avis/Ronna studied various documents.

Then an elderly man approached Cassie and asked her if the library had any books by Richard Grayson. I grinned. "There are two other Richard Graysons," I explained, "and both of them are writers. I tell people their books are mine, and they probably do the same with my work."

I haven't analyzed the dream, but it *feels* very significant, touching on the major issues in my present life.

This autumn of 1978 is taking on a rhythm of its own as I adjust to my routine. It's still an adventure, anyway.

Thursday, October 19, 1978

Noon. I woke up this morning with terrible gripping
stomach pains, the kind I used to get every few
months – probably it's too much gas. So I've been
lying quietly. At the moment the house is empty
except for me.

Why haven't I looked for an apartment yet? Because I
do not want to move out. It's hard enough for me to
get time for my writing, and if I had my own place,
I'd have to cook, shop, clean, do the laundry and a
million other time-consuming (that's not a cliché – I
mean it in its literal sense, *devouring*) chores which
would take up the little time I have.

Last night I spent with my books – what a joy.
Reading alone, I feel more alive and in contact with
reality than I ever do in the classroom. I wish there
were NEA Reading Fellowships; I'd like nothing
better than to take a year off and read, read, read. I
see why writers' colonies are needed.

I'm going to apply to Provincetown again and maybe
to a couple of other places. I need big blocks of time,
and now I don't have that. I've proven that I can be
very productive when I have the time – as I was this
July, for example, when there were no outside
pressures. I want my work to mature.

I've been thinking a lot about "innovative fiction" and how it almost seems to be a dead end. I mean, there just aren't that many ways to innovate, are there? I'm a writer who was brought up on and taught post-modern fiction writing, and most of my work has been non-traditional – but it's also been self-conscious, precious, self-indulgent, form without substance. Right now I want to get back to telling stories; that seems the most important thing.

Jonny wrote a satirical essay for school on "How to Commit Suicide," and I gave him *The Savage God* to read. But Jonny is doing very well; he's not afraid to go out. Last night he took the Cadillac to Bergen Beach and went out with his friends.

My car is falling apart: the heater doesn't work, the shocks need to be welded, oil leaks out daily, and I get strange knocking noises when I make turns. I remember the first day I had that car: it was a shiny god and smelled that fabulous new car smell. I drove it out to Staten Island, and it was a joy. I found Ronna in Clove Lake Park with those kids from Red Hook she was tutoring. Those days seem idyllic now, and in fact, they were.

The only regret I have about my college years is that I cannot live them all over again. The four years I spent as an undergraduate were the happiest, most carefree years of my life. I savored them, but if I had only known that life isn't all college (if you know what I mean), they would have been more precious to me.

Although now I am more sure of myself, I miss the innocence of my college days – not moral innocence but the innocence of what it means to be an adult. I'm resisting being an adult even this minute. (Peter Pan: *"I don't wanna grow up, I don't wanna go to school."* – and I don't; I'm thinking about calling in sick today.)

Oo, my stomach hurts. Last night Gary told me about all the problems Betty's been having with her stomach: nausea, acidity, pain. She's been to doctors, but they can find nothing physically wrong with her. Gary and I know it's probably emotional, but as Gary said, "You still have to alleviate the symptoms."

Pseudo-profound thought: Maybe *life* is a symptom. And it needs to be alleviated. Da-de-*dum*.

<u>Friday, October 20, 1978</u>

6 PM. I'm tired after a full week. I'm glad I prevailed upon Ronna to meet me in Brooklyn rather than Manhattan tonight. My stomach felt much better by yesterday afternoon, and I was able to teach my class. I talked to my freshman students about how they feel about Kingsborough after half a term; most of them

see it as an extension of high school. I do like them
after all, and the affection is mutual.

Even with the more difficult 23 class today, I'm able
to get through at times. So I *am* a good teacher; it just
took time to win confidence in myself at a new school.
The second half of the term should be easier.

Today I got paid, which cheered me up immensely:
$671.63 (about $200 was taken out in taxes). I now
have nearly $900 in my bank account, more than I
ever have had. And 4 weeks from today, I get paid
again, and by then I should go over the $1,000 mark
for the first time.

Today I also cashed a $25 check from Bernhard Frank
of *Buckle*. He thought my piece on Susan Fromberg
Schaeffer was "a joy." She liked it too, apparently.
I'm pleased to know I can write non-fiction well
(though I always knew I could) and that if Baumbach
hates me, I have a friend in Susan.

George wrote me an incredibly delightful weird
letter, ranting on and on about my bright future in the
world of literature. I've spent much of my spare time
in the past two weeks catching up on correspondence.

David Gross thanked me for helping him with his
story. I advised him to send it to Sue Stephens of
Tailings, and she accepted it: his first publication. I'm
really glad I could help. Sue herself sent me a letter

asking for help in getting *Tailings* distributed; I'll see if I can get Laura to stock it in the Eighth Street Bookshop.

Last night I wrote letters to Tom Whalen, Tom Person, George (in two weeks I should be in Harrisburg), Brian Robertson (who's got a writer/teacher position with the Texas Arts Council and who's starting a newspaper humor column), Bernhard Frank (advising him to change the last line of my profile of Susan, which he thought was too gushy), and Douglas Messerli of *Sun & Moon* (I re-subscribed; my "Clumsy Story" will be in the next issue, now at the typesetters).

Yesterday I got a rejection which said, "Your work always leave me with a haunting feeling. Sometimes you seem satisfied with mediocrity, and other times you're brilliant – as in that story about the family ["Wednesday Night at Our House"] . . ."

The editor was right, of course. Maybe it's all to the good that I'm not producing a story a week now. But how it surprises me when people are familiar with my "work." Another rejection said, "...but congratulations on *Disjointed Fictions*." There are people out there who know who I am.

The funniest letter of the past two days was addressed to Mom. Remember that dippy Miss Louisa G. Rogers of *the new renaissance* and how I got back at her for her stupid letter by writing in Mom's name that I'd died? Well, last spring I had "Mom" send her "late son's story, 'Coping,'" to *the new renaissance*.

Today Mom got a flowery letter announcing its acceptance and publication in the spring 1980 issue. They're giving me (or my mother, rather) $40 for the story. I wrote back in Mom's name thanking Miss Rogers and telling her that she, Mom, was now writing stories under the pen name Richard Grayson "as a tribute to my late son." This has to be the best literary hoax I've done. Of course, by spring 1980 I might very well be dead, and then the joke will be on me.

Saturday, October 21, 1978

9 PM. Very unlike myself, I feel happy just to be alive. The past 24 hours have been almost perfect – and I wouldn't want them to be perfect, anyway, because that wouldn't be real life. Everything seems to be going my way for a change. I look forward to the future.

My relationship with Ronna is better than ever; she's an oasis in my life. Last evening was idyllic. I went over to her house at 7 PM, and while she showered, I watched TV and talked to her sister, who soon left for a friend's house. When Ronna came out, she started kissing and hugging me and I didn't want to go out to dinner or to the movies or do anything but kiss and hug her back.

She made us hamburgers for dinner and we had a salad and grapefruit juice, and it was so good, just the two of us in the apartment. We watched some TV and then retired to the bedroom, where we simultaneously undressed each other and got into bed.

It was *lovely* – a word I get from Ronna. I *am* very attracted to her, and being with her like that was heaven. I was able to let go, to be completely free, and she did the same. The intimacy is actually better than the physical release. We play like children, we discuss our lives like friends, and we touch each other like lovers – or maybe like an old married couple. For now, for each of us, our relationship is all we want it to be.

I wish I could have slept overnight with Ronna, but I wanted to prepare for my meeting with Wes today. Her mother and Billy came home from the wrestling matches at Nassau Coliseum just as we were getting dressed. I wasn't embarrassed, nor was Mrs. C.

We all sat around the kitchen table talking. Mrs. C thinks that when Alison's parents come for a visit next week, they should get her out of that apartment.

It's dirty and depressing and too big, and Alison doesn't know how to handle her landlords – when the bathroom sink fell out, she was afraid to yell at them to get it fixed, and as of yet, they haven't.

I awoke with a bad sinus headache today, but I cleaned my sinuses out and got up to Wes's by 12:30 PM. He was sleepy-eyed, wearing an undershirt and painter's pants. God, I'd give anything if I could manage that lithe, casual, rock-star attitude and appearance he has.

We discussed his rock criticism (he's doing a review of Heart, the group Ronna and Phil are seeing at the Palladium tonight), and his father came by to drop off a Canadian book that may be best-seller material. Mr. Strick didn't stay very long, and afterwards we began editing the book.

We bullshitted a lot, and drank coffee, and Wes's friend who designs set (for, among others, NBC soap operas and *Saturday Night Live*) dropped by. Wes is seeing this girl Marla, and they're spending more time together because the guy she lives with, a musician, is out of town on a three-month gig. It sounds like a typical New York affair.

Wes was a bit afraid about how I'd react to hearing about his shooting heroin last weekend, but I was more amused than shocked. He likes needles, he says; I think he enjoys the forbidden nature of it.

We worked very hard on all the stories and I was there for over five hours (I had a Pop-Tart for lunch). Many of my last lines are weak and had to be cut – and we switched things around. There's still about ten more sections that need editing, and I'm going to work on them during this week.

And when everything is finished, we can go into production – hard as that is to believe. I came home exhausted, starved and quite happy.

Sunday, October 22, 1978

7 PM. Another weekend over, and another Monday-through-Friday about to begin. Today was summerlike, 70°, sunny, light breezes – the only problem was that there wasn't enough of it. It's pitch-black now, and that means next week, when we turn the clocks back (we do get an extra hour, though), it will be dark before 6 PM. Ugh. But I shouldn't complain. I'm young, I've got my health, $900 in the bank, a book on the way. . .

Last night I saw the last episode of *The Mayor of Casterbridge*. Butchered Hardy though it was, it got me wondering about the "happiness" I was feeling. Is happiness an illusion in a universe conspiring against us? And Other Questions. Alistair Cooke

quoted *King Lear*, that line about the gods playing
with us and destroying us on a whim.

I went out to Rockaway this afternoon. Feeling out of
shape (I've gotten fat again), I walked up the ten
flights to Grandma Ethel's apartment. Grandpa Herb
and I sat on the terrace and I read Grandma Ethel's
diet; it's so complicated I had trouble explaining it to
her.

Basically, she's forbidden all canned and frozen
goods, most milk products, anything with sugar,
refined sugar or refined wheat. She's supposed to eat
a lot of raw fruits and vegetables (eating the "whole"
of the food, even seeds and skin), legumes, herbs,
bran, wheat germ, nuts and fresh juices. There are ten
bottles of food supplements on the table – a total of 34
pills Grandma Ethel must take every day, all at
different times.

This revolution in her body – "detoxifying," her
doctor calls it – is making her into a nervous wreck
and giving her headaches, stomachaches and
aggravation. But she's probably eating more wisely
than any of us. I think I would go mad trying that
kind of diet.

Grandpa Herb showed me all the money he's making
as a tailor for people in the building, and he insisted
on pushing a five-dollar bill on me – "for carfare." I
ended up taking the money and feeling a bit guilty.

(No, I'm not *really* guilty. That was a lie. I like the idea that my grandfather gives me money almost as much as he does.)

Avis wrote me a wonderful letter in which she apologized for criticizing my book and telling me she would knit me a sweater to assuage whatever pain she caused. Oh, Avis! She's disappointed she didn't get to see Teresa while Teresa was in Europe, and she's anxious to see us when she comes to New York on December 16. I can't wait to see her.

Helmut has tonsillitis again, and he's going to have them removed soon. They've got a houseguest and a new cat, and Avis overdrew her bank account for the first time. Her father is being taken off chemotherapy next month, and that's good news.

I wrote her back a long, breezy letter last night, though I wish I could have phoned her and chatted.

Today was the New York Marathon: 10,000+ people ran, and Mom and Dad went to Downtown Brooklyn to watch the runners pass by (and pass out). The new Polish Pope, John Paul II, was inaugurated today; he seems brilliant and his fluency in in many languages astounds monolingual me.

I just came across a favorable review of a couple of pieces of mine in a literary magazine, *The Smudge* –

well, maybe not that favorable; they said "a decent duo of stories."

There is a conflict in me between my small press loyalties and my New York-publisher dreams. Obviously some small press people will see me as a sell-out. But I refuse to look at it that way. Mr. Strick contacted *me*; I didn't go, hat in hand, begging to be published. As A.D. Winans said, "We all make compromises, whether we want to admit it or not."

And certainly if Taplinger does publish my book, it will do me more good than anything else has. I'm beginning to feel more confident about my work again. I'm young, after all – young for a fiction writer, that is.

Monday, October 23, 1978

8 PM. Today was about the best day I've ever had at Kingsborough. I guess it's because I've finally adjusted to the place. My students are now used to me, the freshmen are used to college, they seem to like me, and I've discovered I like them. And people at the college are familiar to me; I can walk through the campus and hear people call my name.

Today, for example, some girls said, "Oh there's Ivy and Alison's English teacher." Rosa Cordero invited me to her birthday party on Thursday, and since it seems to mean a lot to her, I told her I'd drop by. My lessons went well today, and I felt I was really getting through to my classes. Teaching can be very satisfying on days like today.

It was eerily warm – 76° – and very sunny; it won't be like this again for another six months. Right now a storm is brewing and the temperatures are plummeting.

I went to Kings Plaza at 11:30 AM and had lunch at Bun 'n' Burger; it was a nice change of pace, and it also gave me time to go to the bank. The day went so quickly, and I had so much energy I can hardly believe it. (This is a counter-example of the kind of organized narration I lectured my students on today.) Maybe it's because I stayed in bed until 10 AM, shifting from one delicious dream to the next.

During my break today, I typed up a new vita on the English Department IBM typewriter, and at about 5 PM I went over the Junction to xerox it. I ran into Angie, who's now a Brooklyn College student, and she waited while I had my résumé run off so I could drive her home.

She enjoys college, she says, but it's very hard work; she spends every night studying. Angie's in a special program and goes from 9 AM to 4 PM almost every day, taking all of her courses in one room in Whitehead.

Despite limited financial aid, she's having money problems and she hasn't been getting along with her mother. Angie said she'd like to move out; maybe if she could get welfare, she could swing it.

She also doesn't like running into Chuck. The last time they saw each other, he smacked her; Chuck's just too angry to be friends. His mother, however, spoke with Angie and says she understands how she feels. I dropped Angie off and wished her luck with her studies. I think she'll make it.

Last evening I spoke with Ronna. She and Phil had a good time at the Heart concert; yesterday she spent with Alison, who was sick with her period. (Alison is "very frail" – that's what Midwesterners call a *kvetch*.) Well, ("Avoid *well*," I write on my students' papers).

This is the first time in a while that I feel I have spare time. It's wonderful. It's four weeks since Dad's surgery; he felt dizzy again today, but that's to be expected. Tomorrow is the halfway point of the term, so it's going quickly.

Time does seem to be flowing at a more rapid pace these days. It' almost Halloween, and then comes Election Day, Thanksgiving, Christmas, 1979. Soon I'll have to buy my eleventh of these diaries.

I like this time of year, for some reason. It reminds me of being young. Today, talking to my students and to Angie, I remembered so clearly the fall of 1969, when I was an entering freshman at Brooklyn College. The neurotic in me tells me things are going too well and that there'll be hell to pay tomorrow.

Tuesday, October 24, 1978

7 PM. Today was not the day yesterday was – obviously. For one thing, the temperature dropped into the 40°s. For another, my classes did not go all that well, especially the 3 PM class, who were so rowdy, I ended my lesson in mid-period and made them do a series of busy-work exercises.

I didn't like them very much today. They're so immature. One girl in particular angered me by talking throughout my lesson, calling out irrelevant remarks and then mumbling "Bastard!" and tearing up the C paper I handed back to her.

Kingsborough was an annoyance today, an interruption in my real life. Last evening was real life; it was terrific. I wrote 18 poems, most of them better than anything I've ever written before. It started when I began leafing through my diary from last fall. I found some passages that sounded very good and decided to put them in poem form.

I used all lower-case letters and a conversational tone. I guess reading a great deal of poetry finally paid off. Today I bought envelopes and stamps, xeroxed the poems and submitted them to about 20 magazines – my first real assault on the poetry market. If I get three acceptances, I'll know I've got something and that I really am a poet.

I seem to have found my voice all at once. Of course, it remains to be seen whether I'm considered a *real* poet, but for now, I'm excited by this new development. For months I've been leading toward this; there are some things which never worked in fiction which might work in poetry.

I've had half a dozen poems published so far, but I've never really worked on my poetry. Maybe I should take a workshop. Why am I interested in writing poems now? Maybe it's just a whim, or maybe I need a break from fiction, or maybe I've accomplished everything I want to in fiction – at least for now.

With my book probably being published, I feel the need to prove myself in another area; I want to succeed as a critic, too. Maybe this is just a fantasy, but trying to achieve this looks like fun. And last night I felt just the way I do after writing a good story.

Teresa phoned last night; she'd just received the copy
of *Disjointed Fictions* I'd sent her. She and Mary had a
lovely time in London, and they traveled all over
England and Scotland; Paris was a mistake, for they
found it dirty, dismal and unfriendly. As others have
told me, Europe is crawling with rich Arabs; in some
parts of London, the Rolls-Royces are parked four
abreast, Teresa said, "and they're all dressed like the
characters in a grade-school Christmas play."

Teresa's unemployment (and Mary's) runs out in
February because they shortened the period to 26
weeks (from 39 – when I collected two years ago, the
period was a whole year). I told Teresa I'd come by
late Friday afternoon; my weekend is going to be
crowded, what with Janice's Halloween party on
Saturday night, but I can't spend my whole life
working.

I had told Ronna that I might see her tomorrow night,
but now I think I'd better make time for myself. I'm
having trouble getting everything into 24 hours. Last
night, when I felt free for the first time in weeks, my
creativity asserted itself.

I just wish I had time to read books. The only things
I've been able to read lately have been magazines,
newspapers and poems. I know if I got some kind of
fellowship, I could be terrifically productive. To have
a Guggenheim . . . And it's not the money that's vital,

it's the *time*.   But this is a problem most artists have, and have always have, and *will* always have.

Wednesday, October 25, 1978

11 PM. Today was very hectic. Wesley phoned this morning to say they had a meeting yesterday and they've decided to do my book in the spring. "That means we've got to move fast," Wes told me.

I can barely believe it. When Wes first mentioned them having a meeting, I thought surely they'd decided not to do the book at all. The cynic in me can't understand why the Stricks are so interested in my work.

Anyway, this made my whole day – and the days to come – into nervous times. I wish I could take off a few days from Kingsborough to get myself and my manuscript together.

The less said about my classes today, the better. I resent having to spend time trying to teach kids who aren't interested in learning. Of course, about half of them are really nice, but the other 50% seems to overwhelm the good kids.

I also resent being treated as less than human by the full-time tenured professors. I just wish people recognized me as a writer there. I constantly get mistaken for a student by the professors.

Do I sound obnoxious with all these complaints? Anyway, when I got home from school, I sat down at my typewriter and began revising some of the stories, and I noticed that my letters were fading away.

Immediately I decided to buy a new typewriter. I had my eye on the Smith-Corona Coronet XL with its cartridge ribbon, IBM-style keys, wide carriage and power return. Catching Mom in a good mood, I persuaded her to come to Ciro's with me and pay for it with her MasterCharge.

I'm a cheapskate, of course, and having to shell out $250 to pay Mom back doesn't thrill me, but I need a typewriter more than I need a car or my own apartment or new shoes. I'm sure to get use out of it.

When I opened up the typewriter at home, I found they'd given me one with artistic type, and I had to return it for one with pica type. (While I was there, I ran into Ronna's mother and Billy, who were buying a toaster, a smoke alarm, and a Water-Pic.)

I've been working steadily since 7 PM or so and I really like my new machine. It's no IBM Selectric, but it's good enough for my purposes. In any case, I have to type over two stories that I don't seem to have in typescript, and I'm still waiting for the two stories I don't have at all; Wes sent them out on Monday. He wanted me to come in tomorrow or Friday and I told him I'd be at his office at 2:30 PM on Friday. So, things are happening fast, and there's no time for reflection or poetry.

It's chilly now, but it's almost November, after all. Today I sat by the beach at Kingsborough between classes; it was relaxing, but very windy. I didn't get a chance to exercise today, and I worry that I'm going to become "un-addicted." But this is a special time in my life. If Taplinger does publish my book, it will be the most important of my achievements.

I'll finally be a *real* writer; then I can start worrying about whether I'm all that good. I want other people to know I'm 27 and to get envious the way I did when I saw books by Ann Beattie and Fran Lebowitz. I just wish there was more time in which to figure out what the hell is going on.

Thursday, October 26, 1978

7 PM. I'm feeling rather chipper after a decent supper. Maybe I feel more energetic because I had no meat. They now say it's best to have your lightest meal late in the day, and I think that's probably true.

Or perhaps I feel good because I don't have all that much to do. I rewrote and revised all day today and seem to have most of the manuscript in shape. I feel very loving toward it; it's as though it's my child.

I still do not believe it's actually going to be a book, and I don't know what it will take for that to happen. My name on a contract won't do it; maybe seeing it in the Taplinger catalogue will. Certainly getting the galleys will. I want *not* to think of it, *not* to write about it – because I'm desperately afraid of a *kinnahora*.

Last night I slept like a prime minister; there was this delicious dream of me riding a bike through the neighborhood, not having to pedal, relying solely on a friendly wind.

I awoke and found I had to go to the bathroom; my arms and legs moved so stiffly because of that chemical secreted during dreams which prevents you from physically acting out what you're dreaming.

One of the better things about my present schedule is the luxury of lying in bed at 8 AM and knowing I can go back to sleep for an hour or two. This morning, as I said, I worked on the manuscript. It was dark and mild, a perfect day for a Thursday.

My class at 3 PM was small and they were tolerable – which is to say that I came away not hating them all that much, possibly because I won't have to look at them for three days.

Last Friday, my old linguistics teacher at Richmond, George Jochnowitz, had an article in the *Post* on graffiti. I wrote him, and in reply, I got a very kind letter; he said he remembered me well and asked where he could buy the little magazines my stories appear in. How nice – but he's a great guy.

And I got a rejection from *Zone*, but Peter Cherches asked me if I wanted to contribute to a reading they're doing at the West End Bar on December 10. Maybe I will. Paul JJ Payack sent me a "What's happening?" card. Months ago I promised to a critical article on him.

I feel smug now that I've got a commercial publisher. I do want all the small press people to know about it – which is horrible of me. Some of them will probably say I'm selling out, but deep down I know of few of them who would turn down this chance. But I promised myself I wouldn't write about it! It's hard not to write about the main thing on your mind.

Ah, I'll write about trees instead. The trees in Brooklyn are glorious now; this is the prettiest week of autumn. I especially love the leaves that turn fiery gold and wine-red. I sat on the porch this afternoon and admired the trees on our block. Our own sycamore looks good from a distance, but it's infected with that blight that affects many of the sycamores in New York. Its bark is peeling off and the leaves are tattered and shot through with holes.

I like – maybe I *love* – my new typewriter; I've begun to get used to it. I promise to take good care of it. I wish I'd taken better care of my car, which is now a sputtering heap and looks and acts the part. I don't even know if it will get me through the winter.

Tomorrow I see Wes, and why do I feel impending doom? *The book isn't going to happen,* a part of me keeps saying. Tomorrow night I'll feel dreadful and angry and pour my frustrations onto the next page. (*Kinnahora?*)

Friday, October 27, 1978

7 PM. I'll be going over to Ronna's in a little while, just to hang out and watch TV.

Last night I realized something else about my dreams. I dreamed about a black cat pouncing on me, and the shock of that woke me up. I closed my eyes and I saw an orange outline of the cat, a kind of after-image. So

images are really flashed in front of my eyes when I
dream – or anyway, they seem to be.

This morning I surprised myself by marking eight
papers; that was more than I expected I could. I had
an easy day at Kingsborough, meeting with my
English 23 students individually to get their term
paper topics.

Then I drove into Manhattan to meet with Wes. The
secretary was expecting me, and Wes was having a
meeting with some executive when I arrived. He
introduced me as "one of our spring authors" – he
also did that with another person, who said, "*Hitler in
New York*, right?"   Wes said, "Yes, he's the man who
brought Der Führer to the Big Apple."

He showed me the copy he'd written for the spring
catalogue; it was embarrassingly fulsome hype. But
God – these are all dreams of mine come true. The
book is listed for May, and in his father's office, Wes
assured me we have plenty of time.

He wants to read the manuscript over again and
make any new changes he thinks necessary. It
doesn't have to be at the typesetter until the end of
the year. Then we get the galleys back and the fun
begins.

When Mr. Strick returns from London in late
November, he'll want me to sign a contract; Wes left

all that to his father. I keep thinking something's
going to happen – Mr. Strick dying in a plane crash,
Wes having a falling out with him and leaving the
firm, the whole company being taken over by a
conglomerate. I'm not going to believe it until I see
the book.

Oh, this is torture – exquisite torture, but I can't help
feeling it's not going to happen. I'm going to wake
up and there will be no Louis Strick, no Wes, no
Taplinger, no *With Hitler in New York* (even
underlining the title makes me feel creepy).

When I called Teresa yesterday to cancel our plans for
this afternoon, and I mentioned how I felt about the
book, she said, "I know; you don't want to give it a
kinnahora." You'd think Italians would have their
own word for it, but there's no word like *kinnahora*.

I loved just talking to Wes – about John Irving (he just
finished *The World According to Garp*) and George
Braziller (Mr. Strick is negotiating to possibly buy
Braziller out; he's taken tremendous losses lately) and
just plain gossip.

I love Wesley Strick for what he's done for me; it's not
just that he's cute. Without him, his father never
would have done the book.

I was shaky when I felt the office – Wes said not to
expect to hear from him for a few weeks – so I went to

Brownie's and had orange cake and rose hips tea. Then, at the Eighth Street Bookshop, I noticed that they'd sold another copy of *Disjointed Fictions*.

Back home, I found two neat pieces of mail: an acceptance of "Headline History" by *Nit & Wit*, and a wonderfully friendly note from Mary Stuart, thanking me for sending her a copy of the Joanne Vincente article. She's doing a book for Doubleday this spring and she's excited about it, too.

Saturday, October 28, 1978

5 PM. Tonight is the night we turn our clocks back. It will get dark very early tomorrow, but at least we get an extra hour's sleep. I, for one, can use it. I didn't get to sleep until 3 AM last night because my mind was racing.

I couldn't stop thinking about my book and what it means. Strange thoughts kept popping up. For about half an hour I decided I was in love with Wes – *really* in love – and I became frightened I would make a fool of myself.

In the brisk light of afternoon I realize that I'm confusing a lot of different feelings with love. But Wes and I have worked so closely on the book, I've come to know him very intimately. And he's read just about everything I've ever written except my diaries, so he knows me better than just about anyone else. He's handsome, sexy

(Interruption: there was just a terrible car crash on our block by the Fillmore corner, and I called an ambulance because someone yelled for one. They'd gotten a call already and said they're on their way. A little girl is hurt. God, there have been about 40 accidents on that corner – including mine.)

Where was I? Wes. He's charming, literary, witty, so it's natural I'd be attracted to him. But I'm not in love with him, thank God. Maybe it's easier for me to think of that than to comprehend the reality of my book.

It changes a lot of things for me. It gives me a reason to live through the winter. It gives me hope that I won't have to spend another four years teaching remedial English. (Yesterday I read in the *Post* that the CUNY community colleges have to lay off faculty in the spring because of the tremendous budget cuts caused by low registration, so I might be out of a job anyway.)

And in May, when it becomes warm again, my book will be out. I can't complain that I'm going nowhere. It's obvious, anyway, even without the book, that I'm coming up in the world.

Today's mail brought a letter from Rick Peabody of *Gargoyle*, asking me to submit something else for his special Fiction issue if I want to; an acceptance of "The First Annual James V. Forrestal Memorial Lecture" by *Chouteau Review* (the story will be in the book anyway); a copy of *Another Chicago Magazine* with my "More Fragments" and a contributor's note saying I "play lead guitar with A Small Band of Zionist Hoodlums, which recently played CBGB."

Now in my contributor' notes, I can mention *With Hitler in New York*. I have 120 stories accepted by now, not including about six or seven which will appear in *Hitler* for the first time. And today, in response to *Coda*'s announcements, I sent out another eight submissions of poetry and fiction.

Last night when I went over to Ronna's, her mother was in bed with the flu. We watched the movie *Obsession* on TV. Ronna was very affectionate, but I really wasn't in the proper mood, as I was too keyed-up. I hope to make it up to Ronna tonight, when we go to Janice's party.

Alice is coming in costume; she's meeting Philip, who's reviewing the River Café and refuses to take Alice there in her lion-tamer costume. Last night Janice had an opening at some gallery in Soho; I'd forgotten all about it.

I spoke with Elihu yesterday – mostly talk about being teachers and the gulf between us and our students. And I called Mason, who had a dreadful cold that sounded more like the flu; he's been under a lot of stress and it's no wonder he's gotten ill. At least he doesn't have to face those rotten Rockaway junior high school kids while he's sick.

Sunday, October 29, 1978

3 PM. I'm definitely coming down with a cold or flu, and I must say I've been expecting it. Perhaps I'm even bringing it on subconsciously. When I spoke to Mason the other night, I realized I was feeling a trace of envy. And last night and Friday night, seeing Ronna's mother being pampered and waited on may have also contributed to my wanting to get sick.

I've been under a great deal of stress for the past couple of months; getting used to working five days a week at Kingsborough; then Dad's surgery and hospitalization; then the book for Taplinger. Now that the term is half over, Dad is well and the book is going to be published.

I've let down my defenses. It's a good time for me to get sick. There's nothing pressing this week except my going to the Motor Vehicles Division to fight my summons. I need a couple of days off; this is the middle week of five 5-day weeks in a row, so maybe this illness is my own doing. If so, I'm doing a good job of it.

I woke up with a sore throat and a postnasal drip, which always presages a cold for me. I felt very weak. Upon starting my exercises this morning, I strained that muscle in my chest, and that ended that.

I haven't been able to gather the energy to mark the papers I have to; I have no energy at all. In fact, I'm going to stop here.

*

Half an hour later: I was lying inert until Jonny just came up with a chipped front tooth. He was gritting his teeth while lifting weights. I am from the teeth-gritters myself, and my teeth are also very soft.

My body now feels as though it's been taken over by aliens: aches everywhere. Last night, however, was nice. I picked up Ronna at 9 PM and I can honestly say I never saw her looking more beautiful.

She was wearing a white pullover over a man's shirt, chino pants and high boots. I couldn't get over how well she looked. Her hair was kind of frizzy, and I like it that way.

Janice's party was in the basement, and when we arrived, Dolores and her friend had arrived, dressed as Tweety and Sylvester, Dolores in yellow crepe-feathers and tights and headgear. Janice was dressed as Fritzi Ritz, and someone else was Mickey Mouse.

It was a small party, and I didn't know too many people there, and some of them I did know – like Harry Steinberg the dreary pornographer – I avoided.

Janice roped me into a contest eating donuts from a string and trying not to let the pieces fall to the floor. I lost. I danced with Janice and Dolores, who was on roller skates.

Alice wore tights, a top hat, a bow tie and velvet jacket; she gave me an Icelandic comic book (*Anders And* – Donald Duck) and book of Icelandic short stories.

At *Seventeen*, Alice said, everyone's leaving, and she would like to as well. Macmillan wants to do her modeling book, but only if *Seventeen* puts its name on it. Ray Robinson gave his okay, but now it's got to go through 100 other people.

I got a bit upset when Janice told me what a bad businessman Louis Strick is. She said he doesn't know which direction he wants to go in.

Philip, fresh from the River Café, looked very well. He found Ronna enchanting (that's a Philip word) and told me not to let her "slip away." Philip's show is going to open in January, he sold a children's musical to Boston TV, and will be on *The $20,000 Pyramid*.

Ronna and I drove Philip and Alice to the Newkirk station, then we came to my room and made love. It was silent and very slow; the feel of Ronna's ass muscles moving under me nearly drove me crazy.

Monday, October 30, 1978

5 PM. Last evening, as I began to feel better physically, I also began to sink into a depression. I was feeling very high while reading Kenneth Tynan's portrait of Mel Brooks in *The New Yorker*. I identified like mad with Brooks' outrageous humor, his struggles, his deep suicidal depressions.

It surprised me that as late as 1970 Brooks was, by his own admission, a failure who earned less than $10,000 a year. Now he can do *anything*.

Tynan thinks that the 2,000-Year-Old Man is Brooks' finest creation, and I'm inclined to agree with him. I've heard those records a dozen times and some of those lines are so resonant: "We mock what we are going to become" and the classic "Tragedy is if I cut my finger. Comedy is if you walk into an open sewer and die." (That would make a great epigraph for a book.)

Anyway, I was feeling pretty good until I got a call from Peter Cherches, who wanted to know if I'd donate my time for the *Zone* reading at the West End Bar on December 2nd. I said I would, and we talked for an hour, and when I got off the phone with him, I wanted to die.

For one thing, Peter said *Disjointed Fictions* was very hard to read and shabbily produced. I know it now, and it's mostly my fault; I was so proud of it when it came out and now I'm a bit ashamed of its homemade look.

What bothered me also was Peter telling me about the MFA Columbia program (Hilma Wolitzer teaches his workshop and she can't deal with Peter's stuff, which is similar to mine – she thinks he's just a comedy writer) and small press gossip (how what he called bad poets like Lyn Lifshin, Guy Beining and Susan Fromberg Schaeffer get oodles of credits) and his own acceptances (the same *Aspect* issue I'm in, *Fiction*, etc.)

It made me feel that my work is unimportant, that I'm just one among thousands, and that I may be just another widely-published bad writer. And the Taplinger book probably won't get noticed unless I push it hard.

Let's face it: it's no great shakes and I'll be lucky to get a couple of decent reviews and sales of 300 copies. But I'm going to do my damnedest no matter what. I just hope that I won't have to be ashamed of the work.

I lay inert in bed for hours, not able to sleep. No matter how well I do, it will never be enough, and there will always be people who'll knock me and times when I'll consider myself a failure. I'm a regular manic-depressive, going from fear of superstardom to despair over super-failure.

Why did I choose a job where I'm constantly putting myself on the line? Because, like Mel Brooks, I want to shout, "Look at me!" and "Love me!" and "Don't let me die!"?

I didn't want to get out of bed this morning, and just before I left for school, I had a terrible attack of diarrhea. Somehow I managed to get through my classes, but my mind was elsewhere and my stomach was rocky. (Remember the old days when my stomach was usually rocky?)

I got an acceptance of "The Unexamined Life" by *Scholia Satyrica* that should be coming out next month. Three acceptances in the last three mail deliveries: I can't expect to do better than that, and yet it doesn't satisfy me.

I got responses from Oregon State and Arizona State, and I'll have to send them new dossiers once I have them made up. (More typing, more xeroxing. God.)

I've got 25 papers to grade, but I think I'm going to let it go for tonight. I don't understand it. I'm doing very well, I've never felt more loved (especially by Ronna) or more loving (*ditto* Ronna), yet something's missing.

And it's turning cold.

<u>Tuesday, October 31, 1978</u>

7 PM. Another month gone. Five-sixths of 1978 over. And six weeks from tonight, the term will be over; I can't wait for that. My students are unbelievably immature. Today two groups got into a name-calling match that ended with one student stalking out in the middle of the class.

I didn't blame him. There are loudmouth girls there whom I can't handle. I just wish I could forget about this term. I don't enjoy teaching at Kingsborough and I don't enjoy teaching every day. My students probably don't belong in college at all, or else they need someone with more patience as a teacher.

I'm throwing away all my intellectual gifts and my knowledge teaching idiots third-grade grammar. Ah, well. Tomorrow I don't have to teach. I've canceled my early class, and at 3 PM Carolyn Eckhaus, the counselor, will talk to the students.

I intend to be absent a couple of more times before the term ends. Tomorrow I have to go down to fight my traffic summons. I'm going with the idea of playing a game; I view it not as a nuisance but as a learning experience. The worst that can happen is that the fine stands at $25.

Last evening Michael Kramer phoned. He'd run into Peter Cherches and heard I was having a book published. Michael's stomach problem was diagnosed as an ulcer, and he's had to take it easy. But he's still working for that correspondence school, grading and commenting upon the stories of 200 no-talent suckers.

Joel Agee's book is due out in August, Michael said, and Farrar, Straus is sending Joel to a writers' colony in Virginia to finish it up. I told Michael I'd do something with him on Friday night.

Last evening I typed up a new bibliography, and today I xeroxed that and my dossier and sent it out to Oregon State and Arizona State. But I don't want to live in Corvallis or Tempe.

New York City, it's clear, is going through a renaissance. Despite the financial crisis, or very likely *because* of it, there's a new pride in the city. It's become the international capital, with many Europeans, Japanese and Arabs living here. In the words of the TV commercial, I *do* love New York.

What I think I'm going to have to do to live here, though, is to get out of academia and into publishing. I took out some books on publishing from the library. I think I'd enjoy a job like Wesley Strick's, or even like Alison's at Oxford University Press.

In January and February I'm going to attempt to find a job in publishing or in a related field. After nearly four years of college teaching, I think I've had it.

I've been worrying about signing a contract and I wrote to the Authors Guild to see if I can join. Maybe they can help me; I don't think I need to get an agent at this point in my career – not if I learn everything I need to know.

I've always been ready to totally immerse myself in learning about a field. I did that with politics, and even now my knowledge of electoral facts and figures is stunning (if I do say so myself – I can't wait till Election Day next week; I love watching election coverage).

And I did that with little magazines. I can also do it with any field I'm truly interested in.

Tonight at dinner at Bun 'n' Burger, I thought I saw Mr. Feintuch, Avis's father, but I wasn't sure enough to say hello to him. If it *was* he, he looked terrific.

Wednesday, November 1, 1978

5 PM. November started out mild and sunny. I woke up early this morning and was downtown at 10 AM. I went to the hearing room my trial was scheduled for and waited and waited while Patrolman Terranova charged various defendants with running red lights, driving without license plates, speeding, and other traffic infractions.

One guy got off on a speeding charge because he was on his way to take his dying mother to the hospital. Since she died the next morning, the verdict was not guilty. Another alleged speedster had a smart lawyer and got off.

I noticed Officer Walters and nodded to him. He told me that he was going to ask for an adjournment. Through a clerical error in Albany, the notice of my "not guilty" plea went to his partner instead. Walters, who was in the court on other business, didn't have his notes or diagrams to refer to.

After two and a half hours, my case was finally called. The officer moved to adjourn, and I protested, saying that I had prepared my defense in good faith and taken off a day of work in hopes of a dismissal. He said he was sorry I had to wait, but he was pretty snotty about it.

The trial was adjourned until December 13, the day after school lets out. Officer Walters was nicer than the arbitrator, since he arranged it for a date convenient to me, and we parted on good terms.

I expect to be found guilty, but at least I won't have to pay until next month. It will be the day after the term ends, and I can visit Margaret at LIU that day. (I just sent her a birthday card and enclosed my keys.)

Anyway, the whole experience wasn't frustrating because I took a positive attitude; I took the clerical foul-up wryly rather than paranoiacally.

My 3 PM class was devoted to Carolyn Eckhaus's counseling advice, and she was interrupted by a fire breaking out at 3:45. We all evacuated the building and five fire engines soon came. I didn't see any smoke or flames or reason to stay, so I came home. All in all, this was my best day at Kingsborough.

Time is not as precious a commodity as it was a
couple of weeks ago. I have more free time now to do
some reading – and writing, if I can back to it. It's
been over a month since I've written any fiction, and
maybe I've just gotten out of the habit. More likely,
it's a good vacation for me, and when I do get back to
fiction, it will be with a refreshed attitude. I have my
new typewriter now, and I'm used to it.

There seems little else to write today. I don't *feel*
much of anything: not depressed, not happy, not
intellectually stimulated; I just feel a bit numb.

*

6 PM. I've just finished reading "Goodbye to All
That," the last essay in Joan Didion's *Slouching
Towards Bethlehem*, a book I took out of the college
library because I've wanted to read it for years,
because Didion is such a good stylist, and because I
have trouble writing the third clauses in complex
sentences like this one.

"Goodbye to All That" is about New York, sort of,
and why Didion came and stayed eight years, and
why, at 28, she finally had to leave. I don't think I
want to leave New York, though I've sent out my
dossiers to Corvallis and Tempe.

But New York is only *the city* to me; it's magical but
it's my city and it does not intimidate me and I have

no fancy illusions about it. New York is very
important to me, and I'm glad it's going to be in the
book's title (if there is to be a book – I still have to add
that). Sometimes I think my religion is not Jewish but
"New York" – although, to me, they've always been
the same thing.

Thursday, November 2, 1978

1 PM. Perhaps now is not the time for a diary entry,
but let's find out. Last evening I got terrible diarrhea
again and now my stomach is kind of gurgly. I did
go over to Ronna's, though, because I wanted to see
her. She was still out on her driving lesson when I
arrived. I sat at the kitchen table with her mother,
aunt and uncle. I felt quite comfortable with them,
but Ronna soon came home, saying her right turns are
too wide.

We've been getting closer these past few weeks, both
as friends and lovers. We had an all-time great talk
last night. She asked me if we could go to the 92nd
Street Y next Monday night to see John Irving.
Wesley had told me he was going and I didn't want
to appear as if I was following him around, but with
the suggestion coming from Ronna, it now seems
legitimate.

On Saturday night Ronna told Alice that she thinks
Wes is not just interested in my book, and last

evening Ronna admitted that she is jealous of him even if he's totally straight; she's worried that I'm going to become Manhattan-trendy and shoot heroin.

She said she's been wanting to ask me if I'm in love with him. "I am, a little," I told her, "but it's all so connected with my book." "Well, I suppose that's natural," Ronna said.

I walked her to Flatlands Avenue at 10 PM to buy bagels – it was a lovely night – and then I kissed her goodbye. She didn't want me to drive her the block to her house.

Ronna feels strange now that her friends are getting married next year: Carole to Sid, Helen to Marvin, Alison to her boyfriend Roger (though she's stopped talking about her wedding so much now that she's adjusting to New York).

Yesterday I got an invitation to a gala disco benefit party at Studio 54 on Friday, December 1, from 5 to 9 PM. It costs $10, and Ronna and I are going to go just to see what the place is like and to say we've been there.

At 11:30 last night the phone rang sharply in the darkness. Both Marc and I picked it up and heard a guy say, "Is Richard there?" "This is he," I said, but he hung up.

I lay awake for an hour, trying to figure out who it was. When the phone rang and I first heard the voice, I thought it was Wes because I don't quite recognize his voice yet, but obviously it wasn't he.

I have a strange feeling it was Bobby Mahoney. I think he's very nervous about a possible relationship with a guy. One thing I've learned from answering *Voice* ads is that there are a number of people – Bobby, Bill-Dale, that Robert Lasky – who are having a much harder time accepting their sexuality than I am.

I had a nightmare Tuesday night about Bubbe Ita's funeral; after she was buried, the coffin was unearthed and we had to eat her corpse. Last night I had magical dreams and one frustrating one – I found a little magazine that was supposed to contain a story by me and instead it had one by my old friend Willie Levitt.

Avis sent me a long letter and a photo of herself and Helmut in Bavaria; she looks good with her new frizzy hair. Avis thinks "nothing can stop Richard Grayson from fame, fortune and occasional appearances on the Merv Griffin show."

She was grateful for the newsclips I sent her about the Marathon, the new TV shows, Gig Young's murder/ suicide. She's glad I'm so enthusiastic about seeing her and that I'll have time to do things with her. I've missed her a great deal. Avis has begun to make

hints about trying to live in the Apple again. I almost
wish she doesn't move back, as I like having a
German friend. (Her Deutschmarks are worth so
much more now.)

Friday, November 3, 1978

2 PM. I'm on the verge of a weekend which I've
looked forward to for a long while. I've done
everything that needs to be done and purposely made
sure there are no papers to grade.

I want the luxury of boredom for the next two days. I
want to read, try to write, watch TV, maybe take a
little drive, and I want to remember what it's like to
have time on my hands.

Yesterday I cracked down on my 3 PM class, giving
them a quiz and giving them zeroes for not bringing
their books and generally enforcing rules strictly.
They seemed almost grateful for the structure, despite
their complaints.

I also had a nice class this afternoon. Both classes are
scheduled for finals at 8:30 AM, Wednesday,
December 13, so I won't be able to go for the hearing.
I've decided just to plead guilty and forget it –
probably I should have done that in the first place.

I've been counting the days till the end of the term – there are 40 as of today – but I may find I'm going to be unemployed for a long while. Because of the drastic budget cuts, I'm sure to be fired – or rather, laid off.

Perhaps I can go back to LIU again. Margaret got my card and the keys; I know that because Elihu said so when he gave me his father's regards.

But I'll have a book out next May (I hope, I hope) and I don't have to worry all that much about my future. Maybe it's best that I'm forced to stop teaching for a while and am forced to change jobs.

I was a damned good administrator for the Fiction Collective (they once wanted me to be Coordinator, remember?) and I have organizational skills I put to use in political campaigns, in student government, and serving on college committees.

(This week in *The New Yorker*'s "Talk of the Town," there was an article about Mina Shaughnessy, dean of CUNY for basic skills; that reminded that four years ago I was on the search committee that hired her.)

I've forgotten that I wasn't born to teach, that it's not the only thing I can do.

God, it's a beautiful day: 65° and sunny. This week's weather has been better than I can ever recall for early

November. I bet this winter is milder than last year's, although it would have to be pretty horrendous to be worse. But today snow just seems as foreign as a volcano.

Josh called yesterday; he and Simon may be laid off at the end of the term, too. Elihu bought *Disjointed Fictions* at the Eighth Street Bookshop, and Laura told him to tell me there are only two copies left. Apparently Laura isn't teaching this term; I guess she got sick of freshman comp.

Alice phoned, telling me that Philip couldn't stop raving about how pretty Ronna is – she reminds him of Pam Katz, an ex-student and ex-lover. Alice said that Robert and Judy's wedding in Connecticut was small and tasteful: just a simple synagogue ceremony and dinner at a restaurant afterwards.

Alice sat with Rachel and Mark, who are now living in Raleigh, North Carolina, which is a step up from Syracuse. They've both gotten fat, Alice said, and Rachel looks pretty awful "but she's so sweet." They were impressed with my success, and Alice's – though to us, of course, it's rather a different matter.

George Myers expects me in Harrisburg on Thursday night; I may go down with his friend Stu. I'll probably take the train rather than the bus; I just don't want to screw up my connections in Philadelphia.

So next week I'll only work Monday, Tuesday and Wednesday – which means only one full work week after that, then a short week because of Thanksgiving, two more full weeks, and the final.

Sue Stephens of *Tailings* took "But In A Thousand Other Worlds" and "Look at Our Lives."

Saturday, November 4, 1978

6 PM. I've just come back from the movies. I went to the Seaview to see Altman's *A Wedding*. It wasn't as bad as I thought it would be, but Altman takes such a cynical view of people. I've been guilty of the same thing in my work: presenting characters who are absurd, laughable, yet never quite loveable.

Ultimately we don't care about such people; feeling superior is not a very fulfilling reaction. I'd love to *be* Altman, though, and have the luxury of being bankable enough to have fun with my experiments.

It was dark when I got out of the theater and drove home on the parkway. It's fairly mild, though, and there are piles of fallen leaves everywhere.

As I expected, I'm a bit bored. I haven't accomplished much, although I intend to spend the evening reading Joan Didion.

Last night Michael Kramer and I went out to dinner at Minsky's; it was a pleasant meal, and afterwards we watched TV in his apartment.

Michael is a nice guy, but his bathroom says everything about him. You have to screw in the lightbulb above the sink because the switch doesn't work. Above the toilet tank are his bottles of Maalox and Epsom salts, and he must remove the top of tank and fix some mechanism inside in order for the toilet to flush again.

I got home at midnight. Driving down Flatbush Avenue is scary now; I feel like I'm going through 125th Street in Harlem. They are repaving the street, though, and that's making for a better ride. From Avenue J to Avenue N there are no yellow or white lines drawn yet, and it makes for an almost playful ride.

Last night I dreamed about Hilary Cosell, God knows why. I have an ingrown toenail I managed to butcher, but I hobbled out and visited my grandparents anyway.

Grandma Ethel was sleeping when I arrived; she'd been dizzy, but when she did get up, she looked terrific with her hair cut very short and chic. Grandpa Herb interrupted his tailoring and we all sat around the kitchen table, which had on it bottles and bottles of vitamins, minerals, and whatever else Grandma Ethel takes.

Grandpa Herb told me about his visits to Uncle Jack in the hospital. Aunt Betty had gone away, and they were in the visiting room when suddenly Uncle Jack decided he wanted to leave the hospital. He was attempting to get on an elevator and Grandpa was arguing with him when a nurse came along and asked what the trouble was.

"I want this man arrested!" Jack yelled, and the nurse took him back to his room, playing along and shaking her finger and Grandpa: "Don't you bother Mr. Sarrett anymore!" Grandpa stood by the door of his room and Jack closed it.

Later, when Grandpa came in, Jack again yelled to a nurse, "This man is bothering me! I want him arrested!" And, looking at Uncle Morris, who was sitting by the bed: "And while you're at it, arrest him too!"

Jack likes to sing Russian songs to the black nurses and constantly talks of his mother, which surprises Grandpa Herb: "When Bubbe died, he wouldn't come with me to make arrangements and I had to go with your Grandpa Nat. And though we visit the cemetery all the time, Jack hasn't been there since the unveiling."

This week Jack said to Grandpa, "Momma called and said he was so sick she didn't even take her clothes off at night. She had to go to bed naked." Grandpa pacifies Jack: "How's Tillie?" Jack asks. "Fine." "And how's Abe?" "Fine." "And how's Herbert?" "Fine." "And how is your family? I heard the kids were sick."

Even my grandparents see the awful humor in the situation. "It's pathetic but it's funny," Grandma Ethel said to me. They're trying to get him into a nursing home. "It's terrible in those places," Grandma said. "It's like the Indians – they'd give an old person his things and tell him to go out to the plains and die."

Sunday, November 5, 1978

6 PM. I've just finished reading Joan Didion's wonderful essay, "On Self-Respect." Didion states that self-respect stems from old-fashioned *character* – taking responsibility for one's own life. I don't quite understand all her ideas, but I do feel I am lacking both character and self-respect.

If I had these qualities, why would I have such a voracious appetite for the approval of others? And if I were halfway there, I could accept my tremendous need for "success."

I walked along the pier in Canarsie this afternoon – it was yet another beautiful day – and I watched people fishing dreamily and intently but always *patiently*. I admire their ability to wait; I don't have it, and I'm afraid that unless I acquire patience, my life will be very unhappy.

Here I am in this diary; I can't fool you. People may think that I'm a great success or an egotist or a decent, well-meaning guy, but everything comes down to these pages, where I seek refuge because I can't hide here. I need more discipline and more patience and a great deal more courage.

Rhett Butler told Scarlett O'Hara that people with courage don't require the esteem of others. In a way I see myself as this kind of figure, but in many ways I am not.

Maybe a couple of years ago this would have been a self-lacerating depression, but one of the comforts of growing older is becoming more tolerant of myself. Someday – not too far away, I hope – I may yet become the writer. . . I was going to say "the writer I *need* to be," but what I really mean is "the writer who *doesn't need* to be any kind of writer."

I'm young, and my ideas aren't very complex yet – though they're much more mature than they were.

This morning, shaving, I wondered if writing for me was just a means to an end – success – and that, if circumstances had been different, I would have used politics or acting or athletics to achieve my real goal.

Sad to say, a lot of my need for success is mean-spirited. I simply want to "show up" people who have never believed in me – people like my parents' friends the Cohens, or my Italian neighbors, or the kids who rejected me and ridiculed me.

Often I'm scared at how much I want fame, what I'm willing to do to get it. Like there was a notice in today's *Post* inviting readers to send in on a postcard a list of the ten most important people in the history of New York, and initially I decided (and have not rejected the idea yet) of sending in fifty postcards, each bearing the name "Richard Grayson" at the top of the list.

It's pathetic, I know, and it shows a lack of self-respect, even if I treat it as a game. Success has been so important to me; I've been unable to cope with failure, and that's something I *must* learn to do.

Last night I slept for twelve hours, dreaming of everything – of crying uncontrollably at a funeral, of lusting uncontrollably at a nudist party, of running for blocks and blocks yet arriving too late to prevent my car from getting a ticket for an expired parking meter.

I dread Sunday nights and Monday mornings in autumn. I don't want to go to school tomorrow even though I've been bored for two days.

I finally washed the car today; there was too much birdshit and grime on it for even me to ignore any longer. I've been trying to reach George to find out details of my trip to Harrisburg; I'm looking forward to it more than I am scared of it.

Great-Grandma Bessie is going to Florida with Uncle Jerry, and she's giving up her nice little apartment. I mentioned to Mom that I might like to live there. It's not a good neighborhood, but the apartment is splendid, and it's right by the beach.

I feel a superstitious and neurotic but very real sense of doom.

Monday, November 6, 1978

5 PM. I didn't reach George last night, and maybe it's just as well. Wesley phoned this morning – he always sounds stoned – and said he'd reread the manuscript and made new marks. "The Mother in My Bedroom" needs a new ending, but most of the other stuff is minor.

He wanted me to come in as soon as possible to go over the book with him so we can get it to the copy editor. (Every time Wes calls, I expect him to say they're not doing the book after all.)

I was supposed to go to Harrisburg on Thursday, but now I don't think I will. I can see in a way that I'm trying to get out of it, but that's not really true. Or maybe it is. But it's not important enough for me to get excited over; my book is.

The car broke down today; I'll have to take it to the mechanic tomorrow, which is not a Kingsborough holiday. Why does everything happen at once? It always seem to make that way; for example, it *would* be my summons that got loused up last week and the new date for my hearing *would* turn out to be the time of my classes' finals. I think I'll take off Thursday and Friday anyway; I have many things to do.

Last night I decided not to eat dinner alone, but to go to Ronna's instead. She was at the sink when I walked in and said that second she had just been thinking of me. I wanted to ask her out, but she just insisted on making hamburgers for me and her sister.

It was fun to be out on a Sunday night; I usually spend them dreading the week to come (that's a holdover reaction from public school). We sat in the living room, my arm around Ronna's shoulder, and we watched TV, chatted and kissed. She looked smashing in that white sweater I love.

This morning I worked on preparations for the week's classes and I sat outside waiting for Mom to bring Jonny home so I could drive my car to school. It was very peaceful. A leaf was floating downward from our sycamore tree every few seconds. Jerry came home for lunch. Evie looked to see if the mail had come. Father Marsh strolled by on one of his long walks. It's nice to live in a neighborhood where I know most people.

My classes went painlessly today; I don't mind them if they're well-behaved.

Today Marc went to the bank next door to Jay's Slacks in Flushing when a man tried to hold up a teller. The teller, an off-duty cop, refused to give up money; the robber panicked and shot him; and a detective shot the fleeing robber. Both men died. Marc was very scared, of course, but he wasn't hurt at all. Seeing a man shot in the face must be very traumatic.

Marc just came in and told me the story of his part in the bank robbery. He was friendly with the teller who was killed. Marc noticed that this teller, Mr. Lee, always wore a jacket, unlike the other tellers; he must have kept his gun holster underneath.

Marc was probably his last customer before the
robber tried to hold him up. Lee just took out his gun
and they shot at each other. None of the eleven shots
hit anyone other than the two dead men.

It's just become night now, and the Indian summer is
ending.

Tuesday, November 7, 1978

4 PM. I canceled my 3 PM class, so I'm home early. I
got a lift home with one of the lab teachers and took
the bus from Ocean Avenue to Kings Plaza.

As usual, I'm looking forward to Election night
coverage on TV. There are times when I think I
should have gone into electoral politics, even if I had
to run as a sacrificial lamb as my old BC classmate
Harry De Mell is doing for the State Senate in this
district.

I am cynical enough to know that this election won't
change anything except faces, but I like a good
political race the way some people like horse races.
The numbers flashing on the boards; the restless,
drunken crowds at the candidates' headquarters; the
sense of urgency in the networks' announcement of
projected winners (so that each race is not only a
contest between Democrats and Republicans but also

among ABC, CBS and NBC) – I love all the clichés of election night.

Ten years ago I drove around (without a license) and took photos of people to vote; 1968 was a really exciting and ultimately disappointing election. 1976 was also fun, staying up late and watching Carter win. Off-year elections are less important but often more interesting, as the networks go in depth into each Senate and governorship race.

I walked into the American Legion hall at 9:30 AM and I was the 62nd person in our election district to come out. I voted a straight Liberal Party ticket with one exception: I wrote myself in for Congress.

Gov. Carey, who once looked like a sure loser, has been picking up steam in recent weeks and may pull out a victory.

I tried to call George all last evening but couldn't get him in. Finally I phoned his office this morning; he was out, and I left a message for him to call me, also telling the secretary I couldn't make it this weekend.

In a way I would very much like to go; a part of me hates myself for shying away from another trip. I took the excuse of my book eagerly, so I guess I was a bit apprehensive about Harrisburg. In any case, it's no big deal – or is it? It's another risk I have not taken. Maybe I should have entitled this diary "Risks

Not Taken." But the book has to take precedence over everything else now.

I can't let Tuesday go by without remembering and noting that in another five weeks the term will be over – and so, I expect, will be my career at Kingsborough.

Last night I dreamed about seeing Margaret at LIU; in the dream, they refused to take me back. Yet I don't regret my decision not to teach at LIU this term, as I would have been a nervous wreck by now.

Next week I get another $675 paycheck, and that's worth all the hassle of teaching at Kingsborough – or most of it, anyway.

I finished reading Didion's book this morning. She's brilliant, writing with a stylish ease that belies, I'm sure, much hard rewriting and hard thinking. I would love to write personal essays the way she does – I'm really much better at that than at fiction.

Speaking of fiction, it's been several months, and I still haven't written any stories. I don't really want to. In a sense, my getting a commercial book published was my goal in writing a story a week and hunting out little magazines that would print them.

I've ended a stage in my development as a writer, and now I've got to try to go on to something else – what,

I don't know. Those poems I sent out last month have brought only rejections, so maybe they're not poems at all. I'm searching for a new form, a new voice, and some new themes, and I'm convinced that if I keep living and writing, eventually I'll discover all three.

Wednesday, November 8, 1978

8 PM. Last night was fun for an old election hand like myself. They call the races so quickly now, there's not much suspense, but I like the figures racing on the board, the rush to announce projected winners.

Dad thinks my knowledge of electoral politics is astounding, and I suppose it is. Like everything else, though, it's mostly a matter of studying as much as I can. I can cite percentages and candidates in most Senatorial elections from 1962 on.

I remember being very caught up in the '62 off-year elections. Bill Scranton beat Richardson Dilworth for governor of Pennsylvania; George Romney defeated the Democratic governor of Michigan, John Swainson, who had one arm; Teddy Kennedy was elected to the Senate, beating Speaker McCormick's nephew in the primary and Henry Cabot Lodge's son George in the general election.

In New York that year, the Democrats nominated what *Time* Magazine (my major source of information at age 11) called "the curious candidates": Robert Morgenthau (*Time* said his face always looked like it was cracking apart) for Governor and James Donovan (a lawyer who spent most of the campaign in Cuba, negotiating the release of Cuban refugees) for Senator. They were trounced by Rockefeller and Javits.

It irks me that I can't recall the name of the '62 Democratic candidate for Lieutenant Governor (since then they've been: Howard Samuels, '66; Basil Paterson, '70; Mary Anne Krupsak, '74 and Mario Cuomo, this year). But I'm showing off.

The thing is, governing doesn't interest me all that much. I like *politics* – wheeling and dealing, devising strategy, horse-trading. In the end it's all a game – like last night: there were the usual upsets and squeakers, old faces managing one last hurrah, new politicos mentioned as Presidential hopefuls when in fact they'll be unknown in eight years.

Gov. Carey was reelected, so I was satisfied. The Republican gains across the nation were too small to be of much significance. The GOP will always be able to elect a President, a Governor, a Senator on the strength of the individual, it's lower down on the ballot where most people vote Democratic – when they don't recognize the name, they will go with the party.

Enough about politics. (Yet I can't help thinking that life is all politics, all a wonderful competitive game – that's how I view my literary career.)

I was a bit bleary-eyed this morning; it was a dark, raw autumn day, in contrast to the marvelous weather we've been having recently. (I can't remember a more glorious fall.)

I got through my classes very well today; I was on top of things, felt confident and acted confidently. I was *sharp*. I got Gary's Kingsborough transcript sent to St. John's, as he hopes to start their MBA program in January.

Mom got her first "acceptance" today. A couple of weeks ago I noticed a *Coda* announcement for an anthology of women's "true confessions"; I sent in a piece about Mom almost having an affair with Senator John F. Kennedy and the editors of *Dirty Linen* loved it! They asked Mom to send in more work. Now Jonny, Dad and Marc are jealous and want me to write stories in their names, too.

The police questioned Marc about the bank robbery, but he couldn't tell them that much. The other day Marc told me he feels "trapped" working for Dad and living at home. I think Marc just doesn't like

working, period. (Who can blame him?) Dad says
Marc is silent most of the day while they're together.

I called George and he said that since I wasn't
coming, he would try to get out of the day's work;
he's been very busy at the paper, doing special
promotions.

Thursday, November 9, 1978

10 PM. No one can ever take this day away from me.
Today was the day when – here comes the cliché,
folks – my dream came true. So how come, if I'm
such a lousy writer, I'm having a book published?
Let me crow a little tonight; I promise this will be the
last of it for a while.

This morning Wesley and I prepared the first edited
version for the copy editor. We worked in his father's
office and I agreed to most of the changes; he was
correct in almost every case.

I can't explain how it feels to go to a publishing house
as an author. Mary Walling told me she'd sent my
contract out on Tuesday, hoping I'd bring it today –
but naturally I didn't get it in time. It did arrive this
afternoon, however, after I got back from
Kingsborough.

Today, for the first time, I actually believe the book is going to come out. And it's thrilling: to get a contract in which I'm hereinafter referred to as "the author," to fill out a bio form to be used for publicity purposes; to be able to go next door and tell Evie I'm having a book published and for her to kiss me spontaneously and feel happy for me. I want to share my good news with everyone.

I took the contract to the library, to compare it to what standard author's agreements look like, and I couldn't resist telling the librarian about it – I wish he'd have been more startled. I pointed it out to Joe at the copy center after he'd xeroxed it and he said, "Good luck with it, Richie."

I walked onto the Brooklyn College campus just as it was getting dark. Strolling through Boylan Hall, I hoped I would run into an old teacher so I could show him the evidence of my success. But the corridors were empty, and I realized I didn't need to show anyone – the good feelings were all inside and they couldn't get any better.

For the first time in years, I walked into a LaGuardia Hall, which was almost deserted. The offices are all changed (Student Government is in 160 now, the deans' old complex), disco music was coming over the speaker, there were no chairs in the lobby – but still, it looked just the same.

There are memories in every inch for the place. A thousand moments came back to me all at once, and I started to cry a little. I felt like the hero of "The Eighty-Yard Run" by Irwin Shaw. I looked at *Kingsman* (Kneller is resigning) and the announcements on the bulletin board.

I wanted to tell some students in yarmulkes that I used to be a part of this place. And that there were great people here, and great stories and magnificent times and dreadful times and days that just dragged on. I wanted to touch it all, hoping that would make everything come back to me.

That's why I am a writer, after all – I must record things. "Bear witness," if that's not too pompous. And my next big task is to tell the stories of LaGuardia Hall. Maybe it will be fiction, maybe not – but those times, 1969-1974, are gone now, and someone *must* recapture them.

I walked out of LaGuardia Hall feeling very whole; it was what Maslow (a BC professor himself) called a peak experience.

I phoned Grandpa Herb and Grandma Ethel, and then Josh. I was so pleased to hear he'd sold a story to *Screw* and is writing a lot again. Denis dropped by, and Jerry put him on; Denis likes LIU except for the pay – he told me the people there think I'm really terrific. (Denis said Rose Aronson should be my pres agent.) That made me feel great.

The Authors Guild responded to my letter and invited me to apply for membership. Mikey called and of course asked, "How are you?" I said, "Great," and I meant it.

I know this all sounds like an incredible egotrip, but it's not myself I'm celebrating – it's *everyone*, it's life. I've put my family and friend and neighbors – my Brooklyn, my Manhattan – in my stories, and without all that, I'd be nothing like the self-conscious bore I can see myself turning into.

Friday, November 10, 1978

8 PM. I've just been riding around the neighborhood. Friday night and Successful Young Author Looks Good, Feels Great. But Has Nowhere To Go. I thought of driving over to Park Slope to visit Mrs. Judson, but it's been so long since I last dropped by. Anyway, I could use an early night.

It's November now, but it's unseasonably warm. It's almost eerie, 70°, and crisp, dried-up leaves all over the ground. You could go out without a jacket today. So I picked a perfect day to take off from work.

I wouldn't have minded going into Kingsborough for an hour, but now I feel like I've had a vacation. Of course, it may be the book more than anything else. Today in the *Voice*, I read Richard Price's account of his early success with *The Wanderers* – that was a fluky thing, too, but boy, did he make it big.

I don't expect to be on the Today Show, nor will I have great blurbs (the only ones I could suggest were Susan Schaeffer, Ashbery and Irwin Shaw, who might do it because of my BC connection), and obviously there'll be no movie sale. I doubt if there'll be a paperback sale, but who knows?

I've got six months to prepare my attack on the media. This summer's spree with the Page Six thing was a good dry run, but I'm going to have to go much further. I hope the Taplinger people help me, but I expect to do much of the work on my own.

I spoke to Aunt Arlyne, who books authors for the A&S Hempstead store; she told me of the phenomenal sums publishers spend on Big Book Authors like Marilyn French and George Sheehan.

I won't have access to much money, but I've got idea. For example, I can play up the angle that I was a messenger at the *Voice* to get some publicity there. I can go back to the Flatbush branch library where I worked and ask them to buy a copy.

I've got to get a notebook and fill it with ideas, and I need to make a mailing list of everybody in my family, friends, acquaintances, etc. I feel I can make the book a success.

I mailed out my filled-out bio form and my signed contracts today. Wes said I could call him to find out what's going on; he was going to ask Bobs Pinkerton for the name of a good copy editor.

Anyway, Richard Price said at the beginning of making it, he was Richie In Wonderland. That's what I want to be: a visible public person, someone playing a part in the world. Enough said.

Grandpa Nat went to a group sing-along in the nursing home yesterday. Grandma Sylvia didn't want him to attend, but another resident, a man who has befriended Grandpa Nat, insisted.

Grandma Sylvia watched from just outside the door and she was astounded to see Grandpa Nat remember the word to every song. He sang at the top of his lungs and was obviously enjoying himself immensely. When he left the singalong, he told Grandma, "I've never been so happy. This place is the best place I've ever been."

Hm. Next to that, my ego-tripping sounds pretty stupid. But Grandpa Nat, though you'll never know it, you're a part of my book and one of the reasons I

want it to succeed. Yes, I'm an egotist, but I do feel
I'm part of a community.

That's why I feel a kinship with young writers like
Tom Person (who sent a letter today), George Myers,
Brian Robertson and Tom Whalen. That's why I sent
a check (albeit for only $3) to the Bread Loaf
Endowment Fund – Robert Pack said *any* amount
would be appreciated, and I want to help someone
else get a scholarship.

Saturday, November 11, 1978

9 PM. These last few days have been wonderful. I
feel incredibly relaxed and read to face going back to
school again. And I've got only one more month at
Kingsborough, and that should be easy to get
through. Tomorrow I have marking and preparing to
do, but the work won't be that much.

I spent today with Ronna. It's been difficult getting
ahold of her these past few days. On Thursday night
she went to a play with John, his lover Andrew, and
John's drama class and didn't get home until 1 AM.
I told Ronna's sister to have her call me, but I wasn't
very coherent when we spoke.

Last night she went to the movies with Brad, and then
out to eat with Susan and Marvin. Today she was

going to meet her friend Debbie and her mother, who had taken a bus in from Harrisburg; Ronna had gotten them theater tickets and was meeting them at Radio City to give them to them. (That's terrible construction, isn't it?)

Anyway, I took the D train and arrived at Radio City one train ahead of Ronna. I could see her thinking as she walked up the subway steps, "That guy looks like Richie – it *is* Richie." We gave Debbie and Mrs. O'Hara the ticket and I was introduced, and we walked down to the Smokehouse for lunch.

Debbie is a tall, gawky, very sweet girl who's obviously very close to her mother. They were very nice, unassuming people; they talked about the autumn beauty of Harrisburg and the goings-on in the area.

Mrs. O'Hara very generously paid for our lunch. I tried to protest and finally she let me leave the tip. They wanted to go to Lane Bryant, so we took them to Fifth Avenue and pointed them in the right direction.

Ronna will see them next week (charter buses run from Harrisburg to New York every Saturday) and maybe on her trip to Harrisburg tomorrow.

Ronna wanted to buy a blouse, a belt, a shirt and shoes for her interview with Saul Kohler, the *Patriot-News* editor; she already has a jacket. So we walked to Bloomingdale's, and there we were, Ronna and Richie, another couple in the Saturday shopping crowd at The Store. Ronna found a gray flannel shirt but couldn't find any of the other accessories. We looked in Alexander's, Fred Braun and The Gap.

I liked being with Ronna, but the crowd were giving me a headache and finally we decided to take the train back to Brooklyn. At my house, Ronna and I relaxed, drank soda, looked over my students' very funny (unintentionally, of course) papers and whispered in each other's ears.

I'm very fond of that woman – in fact, I love her, and it's hard to imagine her not being a part of my life in some way. These past few months our relationship has gone extraordinarily well, ever since we decided it couldn't go anywhere.

I'm terribly attracted to her, but I'm terribly attracted to other people, females as well as males. Right now things are just perfect between us. Our relationship has come a long way from our first date nearly six years ago; even on that night I knew she was special.

I like to make her laugh, I like to feel the small of her back, I like her honesty. When we went to Kings Plaza, where she did buy shoes, a blouse, a belt and panty hose, she told a shopgirl she weighed 143. Incidentally, the salesgirl said, "You two must be a lot of fun to be out with." Ronna and I looked at each other and denied we *were* a couple. But we do have that easygoing banter that couples have – yet we don't have the tension, usually.

I left her at her house an hour ago; she wanted me to stay for dinner, but the chicken looked unappetizing and she had to prepare for her trip. I hugged her good night and told her to have a successful interview.

One of the bright spots in my life has been my relationship with Ronna. She says she's always had faith in me, but I think she's amazed that I really I made it as a writer. Well, I am pretty amazed, too.

Sunday, November 12, 1978

1 PM. To be in the house with my family on a Sunday is a reminder of how much I need to escape and how desperately I need the book to succeed. While I've been making much of the fact that ten years ago I was a complete failure at 17 – a compulsive, frightened, homebound agoraphobic – and now I am about to have a book published, I have left out the part that says I still haven't gotten out of this room and this house.

Whatever its virtues, *Hitler* is the book of a child – a precocious one, to be sure, but definitely a child. I am, at 27, neither a "family man" nor independent, and this must change. Perhaps now would be the best time to leave. My car is on it last wheels, and an apartment near a subway station might be what I need.

My mother told me today, "Hang up your jacket," "Dust your room," "When you're in my house, you'll do as I say." I simply ignore her. If she doesn't see what an absurd situation it is, I do. Or maybe she's just being difficult in order to get me to leave.

Anyway – I'll have about $1200 in the bank as of Friday's paycheck, and that's enough for me to start looking next week. My advance should cover a couple of months' rent.

The term is winding down and I'm not all that busy. I haven't been able to write. *Correction*: I haven't *needed* to write, and I suspect that I've simply run out of material. Living in my own place will probably give me a new perspective, and even if it doesn't, I'll still grow personally.

The book changes a lot of things. I no longer have to strive to be published in every little magazine there is. Indeed, my shelves of little magazines with my own stories will seem almost beside the point when my book comes out. What do I need eight copies of *Writ* with "Joe Colletti" if it will appear in my own book?

I'm no longer scared of living alone, so what better way to close the book on the ten years since my breakdown than by finally moving out? The publication of the book signifies my worth as a writer; now I need to signify my worth as an adult male.

My stomach hurts, but damn my stomach. If I don't leave 1607 East 56th Street, Brooklyn, New York 11234, the book won't mean a damn thing.

*

4 PM. I've just gotten off the phone with Mason, who's really in a bad way. He's so miserable at that damn school. He took off Thursday and Friday and went upstate, yet it wasn't good enough for him.

He went to the Crystal Run School, though, and there the retarded residents immediately surrounded him with gestures of deep affection – such a contrast to the hostility and tension of the junior high.

Mason would like to leave, and I was encouraging him to do what's best for himself. He can't allow himself to get sick and depressed; the money isn't worth it.

But of course he feels like a quitter and a failure leaving the job, and people will tell him he's crazy for "walking out on such a great opportunity." He says his parents have been supportive, though, and I told him to do what he wants and not let other people judge him.

I wish I was rich and famous so I could help Mason and Ronna and Avis just a little. Our lives – I told Mason that thirty years from now we'll all look back on this and say, "Thank God I'm not that age anymore."

Monday, November 13, 1978

7 PM, still Sunday – but I *must* write. I have always hated November Sundays – dark, dreary days like today – and I will always hate them. This weekend, which started so triumphantly, has left me feeling defeated and suicidal.

I just came home from The Floridian, where I sat at the counter and had a Western omelet with tea and toast. My waiter had an earring. Probably gay. Despite the defeat of the gay rights bill in the City Council this week, we also had the rejection by California voters of the anti-homosexual teacher initiative and also an affirmation of gay rights in Seattle.

Too bad my problem isn't being gay. I wish it was that simple. Though if I killed myself, as in the Michael Lally poem, "they'd say it was because I was really gay – or because I wasn't really gay." No, my problem is being human."

If therapy were the answer, I'd somehow find a way to get back to it. But as a veteran of eight years and $10,000 worth of therapy, I can readily attest that it's not The Answer.

Oh, it helped me an awful lot, but it can't change *life*, and despite the pep talks of Dr. Wayne W. Dyer and the other pop psychologists whose paperbacks line drugstore racks, life *is* the problem.

Then is death The Answer? I've always suspected it might be. Much of my fear this year has dealt with the possibility of my regressing to ten years ago. Now I see that it's also a *wish* for that kind of pseudo-suicide.

Back in 1968, I didn't take my life, and I'm very glad I didn't. So I probably shouldn't do it now. But still, I've discovered that the book doesn't make me a success; in the eyes of the world – damn the world, *in my own eyes*, I'm a failure.

I may have a book of short stories published at age 27, but I've paid an exaggerated price for that. I've never had a home of my own. This house is not my home any longer. It can't be.

Today I saw a beautiful studio apartment on East 66th
Street and Avenue N. It was perfect: modern, cozy,
magnificently laid-out and decorated. The landlord
was young and friendly and wanted no lease. The
place was so beautiful I came home ready to give the
landlord a $200 check for security.

Then, later, I took out a pencil and began figuring: I'll
have $1200 in the bank as of Friday, but my only
income for the following three months will be a
paycheck in January. $1950 minus $1000 for four
months' rent plus one month's security – that leaves
me $950 for twenty weeks. Which means, taking off
$50 for a phone, I'd have $45 a week to live on.

I couldn't get by on that *now*, and now I don't have to
buy groceries or toilet paper or other household
supplies. I need about $75 a week to live on at
present. And of course all this goes along with an
assumption that I'd have eight credits of classes at
Kingsborough in the spring, and that's not likely,
considering the budget cuts.

My mother looks at me in disgust and says, "When
are you going to get a job? How long is this going to
go on?" My father says nothing, stares at me. I don't
blame them. If I had a son my age who was doing
something I didn't understand, I'd behave the same
way.

So why, with no money for an apartment, do I send $3 to the Bread Loaf Endowment Fund and $5 for some books by *Samisdat*'s Merritt Clifton, a writer who loathes my work?

Because in literature I find the home I don't have here, perhaps. My contract with Taplinger has a clause which states that its provisions will be in effect for my heirs. I wrote Mr. Strick a letter naming Ronna as my literary executor in case I die before the book comes out.

In a way, with the book coming out, I don't need to go on living. For months I've been postponing suicide until the summer session ended, until Dad's operation, until I was sure the book was going to be published.

And now? I want to see Avis in December and Grandpa Nat in January.

Tuesday, November 14, 1978

8 PM. I haven't written in my journal for 49 hours; probably it was a good thing that I didn't write yesterday. As I expected, Mom was very cross me with me Monday morning. She told me, in that very hard way of hers, that she want me out of the house.

I tried to explain to her that I couldn't afford the $200 a month rent and then have money left over to live on, but she continued to abuse me until I broke down completely, crying and throwing myself.

I ran out of the house and into the car, screeching away. In the car, with the windows closed, I sobbed like I haven't sobbed in years. "I want to die!" I kept shouting, and I meant it. I tried to drive with my eyes closed so I would get into an accident, but I was too afraid to do it for more than a few seconds.

At the Marine Parkway Bridge I was stuck as the drawbridge went up. I just sat there crying and moaning and feeling my throat beginning to hurt.

When I returned home to have breakfast, Mom went about her chores, acting very coldly. (Maybe if Maude had come in, none of this would have occurred. Maude's presence puts our family on better behavior. But Maude's mother was ill yesterday.)

I again tried to explain to Mom the situation of my finances; she couldn't understand how I spend $75 or $80 a week and told me I must cut down my expenses.

At that point I broke down again, blubbering about how I have nothing, that I haven't bought a new pair of shoes in three years, that I have no clothes. Mom asked me how my friends managed. "Maybe I made the wrong choices," I told her. "I wanted to be a writer. That was the important thing. So I made sacrifices. I'm sorry. I wish I were dead."

Finally Mom couldn't take my crying any more, and she became sympathetic even though she suspected I was acting – but I wasn't. I was saying to her the things I said to myself in this journal on Sunday, and I believed them then.

I don't believe them totally now – in a moment of routine tranquility – but they gnaw at me. There is a price I've paid for my hopes and ambitions. So forgive me if I toot my own horn too much; I've given up a lot, and I need to believe that I've given up things for a worthwhile goal.

I spoke to Wesley yesterday; the manuscript had gone off to the copy editor (with a style sheet of my grammatical quirks) that morning at 11 AM – just the time I was contemplating suicide.

Wes was very excited. "Your virgin editorial project," I said. "We're losing our cherry together," he told me. Bobs Pinkerton, the managing editor, had taken the book over the weekend and was impressed – and she looks like a hard-bitten, I've-seen-it-all type.

Wes said he liked my bio sheet and told me he'd sent me a package in the mail: "an early Chanukah present." "Thank you for everything," I said.

"Thank *you*," Wes said. "I didn't do anything. You did it *all*." That, and a letter from Wayne State telling me they're considering me for a job on the basis of my vita, helped me make it through these past two days.

That, and work – and I began, as I promised Mom, to clean up my room. Last night I threw out letters, postcards, memorabilia, junk; it was very painful, but I can't keep birthday cards from 1972 forever.

And the four classes I've had yesterday and today went reasonably well. I still can't help counting down: four weeks from today, it will be all over but the final and the final grades.

Wednesday, November 15, 1978

10 PM. Walking by my parents' bedroom just now, I overheard Mom tell Dad, "It went by so fast." Sticking my head in, I asked, "*What* went by so fast?"

"Our years together," Mom said. "We were just teenagers going together, and our parents seemed so old, and now. . ."

I finished the thought: "And now *you're* your parents." Mom nodded.

Life does whizz by. That's why I'm taking off
tomorrow; I need to catch up with my life. There's so
much just to read and people to call and see. I never
seem to get my life in order. My classes are so
enervating, and it's rare when I feel I'm stimulating
my students to any thinking.

Luckily, I've made friends with the other adjuncts,
and talking to them (mostly commiseration) helps
pass the time. The best parts of my day seem to be on
the telephone or in the mails.

Today I got Wesley's "CARE package": a copy of
Taplinger's book *As My World Turns* by soap opera
star Eileen Fulton and a proposal for a book on
circumcision. "We need photos," Wes wrote, "so
please send them along with your facial shots."

He's a darling; I'm glad we get along so well. Wes
has taught me a great deal. For example, I now notice
things I didn't used to.

For example, Carolyn Bennett sent me her Seagull
Press book, *The Last Detective* by Richard Vetere. It
was a wonderful, haunting novella (I must write
Vetere), but I found many errors an editor should
have spotted: In one chapter, somebody goes to a bar
on Sixth Avenue and then takes a cab to a
whorehouse "over on Sixth Avenue." In another
section, a transatlantic flight arrives at LaGuardia
Airport rather than Kennedy.

Josh phoned yesterday and invited me to a reunion of
the writing class that Simon has arranged for
Saturday night at Henry's End; everyone will be there
and it should be fun. I'm the most successful, of
course, but I'd better not try to put on any airs. Simon
wouldn't even call me himself, so obviously, inviting
me was mostly a duty. Perhaps they even hoped I
had other plans.

I spoke to Alice, who's spending Thanksgiving with a
friend in Boulder. She's flying to Colorado with
Richard Sasano, who's visiting his brother there.
(Steve's getting married to an English girl and
moving to London.)

Peter Cherches phoned to tell me the West End
reading has been postponed until January. We had a
wonderful chat about the MFA biz; he's so disgusted
with Columbia but figures he's "buying a name
degree." Most of his classmates in Hilma Wolitzer's
workshop are into "passionate realism. . . *Redbook*
fiction. There's no concern with language."

Ronna and I spoke last night. In Harrisburg, Saul
Kohler took her out to lunch and treated her like a
Dutch uncle. He told wonderful reporter stories; he's
been in the business a long time, covered the White
House for the *Philadelphia Inquirer*, and was press
secretary to Sen. Hugh Scott.

Kohler gave Ronna places and names all over the Northeast and South; he urged her not to specialize right way and to get on a medium-sized paper where she can learn to handle everything. Ronna got out a bunch of letters last night, and Kohler said he'll give her more contacts if need be.

He's a very sweet man; he wants to help Ronna get started because someone once did the same thing for him. It will be a struggle for Ronna, but she really wants to be a reporter.

The Mississippi Mud arrived in today's mail. It's a beautifully laid-out magazine, and my "18/X/1969" read really well.

I spoke to Teresa and she had a delightful lunch with Costas; they reminisced about college and were both surprised at the fun they had. So they're friends again.

I applied for jobs at Arkansas (ugh) and Princeton (hoo-hah).

<u>**Thursday, November 16, 1978**</u>

9 PM. I didn't catch up very much today. I can't seem to get ahead of myself.

Dad called us all in for a conference this afternoon. He's been drawing a salary of $500 a week from the business, and it isn't enough to live on. He felt completely humiliated and degraded confessing that he can't make ends meet.

"I've been taking tranquilizers day and night," he said. "I don't know whether to kill myself or what." Dad said we must let Maude go, or if not, Mom has to get a job (which might be good for her, to get out of the house).

I immediately offered to give Dad $50 a week and told him it was the least I could do. At first he was reluctant to accept it, but it's certainly only fair. It will make me feel better anyway. Marc can contribute something, and maybe Jonny can get an after-school job, though I doubt he will.

Jonny still doesn't know about going to college next year, but what kind of job can he get? As Dad said, neither he nor Marc are professionals, and they're in a terrible situation.

The trouble with Dad's finances is that because he was always in business for himself, he got used to taking whatever money he needed. The family has never lived on a budget, and even now Mom and Dad have no idea how much they spend each week on food, insurance, clothing, etc.

I've been limiting myself to $75-$80 a week, although lately I've been spending more. I've got to cut down on expenses. Hopefully, I'll begin to earn some really decent money next year. As it is, I have twice what I had last year at this time, so I can make do.

In a way I'm glad I can help Dad and Mom out in a crisis. They have almost no savings left – in the past three years, Dad has eaten into almost $45,000. Inflation is partly the villain; it's hard to comprehend when they give cost-of-living figures on the TV news, but it hit home when I looked at Dad's pained face.

That decides it for me: I'm going commercial and I'm going to hype my work or whatever I have to do to get us out of this mess. Otherwise we're going to go under. Everyone predicts a recession in 1979, and some say it could be worse than 1974-75.

My making it will be the best hedge against an uncertain economy we could have. I can't let my family down. Damn *Art* – at least until we can afford the luxury of it.

Today I got a check from Ideal Publications: $30 for "Specialized Soaps." And tonight I found it in a two-page spread of *TV Dawn to Dusk*; they didn't give me a byline, though.

I also got a new story in *Waters Journal of the Arts* – "Different Places" – they handled it beautifully. Too bad it's the last issue "due to inflation."

I've written almost nothing in three months and I feel almost no pressure to write. This half of the year I look on as a vacation, not a writer's block. I have to redirect my writing goals now that I've reached the point of having a commercial book published (I just got a horrible flash: *What if they don't do it?*).

I went down to the Motor Vehicles and changed my plea on the summons to guilty. As it was my first offense, they fined me only $15. My car can't last much longer, and when it dies, that ends my driving years.

It's strange, my having been poor (financially) for all these years. I still don't *feel* poor, yet my room and clothes are shabby, and I don't have much tangible hope of a wealthier tomorrow.

<u>Friday, November 17, 1978</u>

2 PM. It's a very rainy and chilly Friday afternoon and a good time to take a nap. Our remarkable fall weather has ended; now it's winter-jacket rime. In another month or so, it will be snowing and freezing.

But I do have a reason to look forward to spring this year.

I've just come back from Kingsborough, where I had a pleasant session with my 23 class. Earlier this morning I went to school to pick up my paycheck. I deposited it in the bank, but I had to withdraw $300 to give to my parents: $250 to pay the bill for the typewriter and $50 as part of my first weekly payment for household expenses.

I got my photographs back. Most came out poorly, but I sent one black-and-white head shot to Taplinger. I look very boyish, I suppose. I wrote Wesley, thanking him for the book he sent and mentioning his article on Heart in this week's *Rolling Stone*.

How do I feel? All right, I suppose. I'd like to start writing again, but I don't feel desperate about it. I feel I've earned the right to take this breather. Today Pat Griffith of *Washington Review* accepted "Super-Fab Senators" and told me to send a bio note noting "how many thousands of stories you've published by now."

Maybe now I can live off my reputation for a couple of months. I don't know. I have $1005 in the bank now, but it will be eaten up fairly quickly now that I'm giving Dad money every week. I might take a full-time job; I think maybe now I can.

I don't have to prove myself as a writer anymore, and
I could probably take a job in publishing until I can
find a full-time academic position. Yesterday I
answered an ad in the *Voice* for an editorial assistant
at a confession magazine.

Next month and in January I can test the waters of the
job market. I've had nearly four years' teaching
experience, and maybe it's time to more on to
something more profitable. If I *loved* teaching, I
wouldn't consider it, but I'm only half-satisfied with
my present job.

I've been applying for every academic job, and if I get
hired, I'll have to go. I can't afford to pass up any
opportunities, be they in Arizona or Arkansas. I've
applied to writers' colonies, for grants (it's obvious
I'm not getting a CAPS award; they would have
written me for extra copies of my manuscript if I were
a finalist), for readings – for anything that will help.

Sooner or later all this work has to pay off, doesn't it?
Anyway, I'm reconciled to living at home for a while.

Tonight I'm seeing Ronna. I was just thinking that we
don't fight anymore, so tonight we'll probably argue
for hours. But there's not really much to argue over.
I'm very fond of her, and for the first time I think that
if I weren't gay, I'd marry her.

Of course I am gay, and I've accepted that, even subconsciously: in a dream last night a woman accused me of being a homosexual and I said, "I am. So what's wrong with that?"

What I like about being gay now I being able to walk down the street in this neighborhood and see an attractive guy and look at him and his earring or whatever and realize he's gay, too.

I will probably always love women (always Ronna?), but I will always be gay. I answered a *Voice* ad from a gay guy, 22, who's a big boxing fan. I feel glad to know there are gay people who share my interests like that.

I've gotten fat in the past couple of months, and I've got to work hard to become slimmer. I want to look great next spring. At Brooklyn College yesterday I ran into Ken Charters and then Ellen, Ronna's cousin. Both had heard I was having a book published, and Ken said, "You're a popular guy. Everyone at LIU talks about you." One day even more people will.

Saturday, November 18, 1978

4 PM. The sun is low in the sky now, but it's fairly mild out. I didn't enjoy the day because I feel pretty grungy. I didn't get to sleep until about 4 AM and

woke up (just barely – I'm still not sure I fully have) at noon. I didn't shave today. I'm a day person, and staying up late, no matter how much I sleep, makes my eyes very tired.

Tonight I have the MFA class reunion, but I'm not sure I'm going. I'll see how I feel. While it would be pleasant to see the class again, I'd rather not stay up late again, especially since I told Teresa I'd come over tomorrow. I have about 15 papers to mark and lessons to prepare, and I didn't get much accomplished today.

Last night I went over to Ronna's at 8 PM. Her sister had a bad cold but was going out dancing anyway, much to Ronna's dismay. Ronna and I drank Diet Pepsi in the kitchen and made out furiously in the living room; we were rougher with each other than usual.

Then we watched a bloated Liz Taylor in some dumb TV movie, and at 10 PM, when Barbara left, we went into the bedroom. Susan, who has the world's worst timing, took that occasion to phone from Marvin's house.

I was undressed in bed already, but Ronna had only her socks off and was going on and on about some office intrigue. I tried to take it casually at first, but as the minutes passed, Ronna kept chatting on and on. I began to feel ridiculous, so I put my clothes on and told Ronna I was leaving.

Still she didn't bother to hang up. I walked outside, where Barbara was waiting for her friends to pick her up, and finally went back in. Ronna was crying but still talking to Susan.

When she finally hung up, I told her how I angry I was; I *knew* she wanted to cut off the conversation and she couldn't do it. Maybe it was childish of me, but I took it as a form of rejection. And of course now Susan has even more reason to think I'm a stinker – not that she needs any.

But we forgot about it quickly and made love – earnestly, only nothing was going quite right. Finally I suggested that Ronna and I both masturbate; she was hesitant about it, but it worked. I think we were both a little annoyed with each other and not admitting it.

Ronna said, "Just when I think I'm getting deeply involved with you, you show me why I shouldn't." And that's good, as far as I'm concerned. At this point I'd almost rather be friends and forget about sex.

I'm very, very fond of Ronna, and when her mother and Billy came home from wrestling, we sat around the kitchen table and talked for an hour. I loved that, but it was a mistake, because I feel so tired now.

Today I got an acceptance from *The Smudge*, a great little magazine. They asked me for a photo, and now I have plenty. I must now have more than 130 stories published or about to be published. And Elizabeth Janeway sent me a letter welcoming me to membership in The Authors Guild.

Every day this week the mail brought another delight. Things are going so well, I'm almost scared. Kurt Nimmo, the editor of *The Smudge*, says he's going to review *Disjointed Fictions* – favorably, I assume. So I feel light years away from my old classmates in the MFA program. If I don't show up, they'll probably think I'm a snob. And maybe I am.

Sunday, November 19, 1978

7 PM. In an odd way, the more I write, the harder writing gets. It now seems less mysterious than ever, yet it seems to be more work. Most of what I write is garbage, and that realization has made me re-think my whole attitude toward writing.

Even teaching remedial composition has made me more conscious of my worst mistakes – especially misplaced modifiers; overuse of "really," "only," and "just"; occasional dangling participles; and a fondness for gimmickry.

Working on content is just as difficult. I attempt to sharpen my mind with reading, but there never seems to be enough time, and I end up with the merely obvious. My concerns are too narrow and too superficial. I have almost no capacity for critical theory or abstract thought of any kind.

Yet, having accepted all of this, I have to say that I *am* a writer (no, I don't need membership in The Authors Guild to confirm this) while most of those who claim to be are not.

All this is apropos of the MFA class reunion, which I dragged myself to last evening. Actually, it woke me up and made me feel alive on an otherwise dead day. I enjoyed seeing my old classmates as a group and speaking with them individually. But I'm aware now, if I wasn't before, that I am a writer while they are not.

Simon, the most talented of them, has given up completely. He couldn't survive the criticism of the writing workshop, so how could his ego come up against editors in The Real World? I feel badly for Simon's writing, the work he might have produced. But Simon is a schlep; he now tutors at NYCCC and works as a short-order cook on weekends and hasn't written in years.

Sheila never was a writer and she admits this. She enjoyed working in advertising, could have had a future as a copywriter and potential editor at Avon Books, but she took a job teaching at Grady H.S. because she would have lost her license had she turned it down.

Josh will never be happy; one suspects he wishes to make a career out of being unhappy. He likes to think of himself as a rebel and a punk; wants to get into advertising; has bright ideas but always seems to defeat himself. Josh says he's writing, and he might have commercial potential if he straightened himself out.

Todd is of the Old School, like Hemingway – a writer of careful control, "true sentences" and outworn clichés. He doesn't realize that the Hemingway model was obsolete even for Mailer's generation; no one takes hard-drinking, competent, hairy-chested writing seriously anymore.

Todd has only one story: his own, and while it's a fairly good story, it won't set Manhattan on fire. But Todd has a wife and baby and a house, so he doesn't need it so badly.

Denis has little talent but the most ambition. He wanted to find out my "secrets" of "successful marketing," etc. Denis wants to be an academic and he may make it, but he's terribly unsophisticated ("I don't understand poetry," he told me. "Not at all.") He said he admires my single-mindedness and was heartened to know that I doubt myself at all times.

Of course they are all kind-spirited, friendly people: good companions I want to see again, much like the people I met at Bread Loaf. It was actually a delightful dinner, and I enjoyed it, and I even liked driving Simon and Sheila home.

But although I haven't written a story in two months, I am a writer and they are not. This is not in the way of self-back-slapping, but to keep me from despairing in the face of my own failures, my own lack of sophistication, grace, and discipline.

Monday, November 20, 1978

5 PM. Three more weeks and I won't have to look at my students anymore. Granted, most of them are nice kids, but a few have them ruin it for everyone.

When I arrived at my 23 class this afternoon, Rosa Cordero and John Petrowski were bickering; the other day they actually slapped each other in class. "Two-timer," the retard John calls Rosa, and she says, "Shut up."

"All right," I say, "let's try to behave like adults here."

And Rosa yells out, "Teacher, you shut up, too!"

I said nothing but gave her an icy stare – which didn't faze her a bit. By now I think Rosa is psychotic. She's told me some incredible lies, which at first I believed (like her cousin drowning his four kids). I figured people she knows must be insensitive, violent, and lacking any idea of what life is about.

But last week she told me some whoppers. She was in an accident with her cousin, who died but whose baby was still living inside her. Then she introduced me to a girl she said was her younger sister.

"But last week you told me you were the baby of your family," I said. She explained that she'd just met her sister that week; her mother had surprised her. Supposedly the sister had been living in Puerto Rico all these years, unbeknownst to Rosa.

"But why didn't they ever tell you about her existence?" I asked. The answer: "She was very sickly and not expected to live, so they didn't want me to get my hopes up!" And it turns out this "sister" has been attending Kingsborough all along.

I hate the fact that I have to teach such scum as Rosa Cordero. I'll pass her because she's already threatened me if I don't. Anyway, I've got to concentrate on the well-behaved, earnest students who (even at Kingsborough) seem to constitute a slim majority. But yesterday I scanned the want ads for jobs in publishing and other fields.

Wesley phoned today. I always think he's going to say they can't publish the book after all. But it came back from the copy editor, who did a very good job. There were some "flags" – questions on yellow paper that the copy editor attached – we had to go over: the title of Bishop Sheen's book, the spelling of *Farshteit*, etc.

Now I just have to think up half-titles before we can go into production. I've decided to use story titles as half-titles, but that means changing one of the titles in the "Women" section. I told Wesley I'd phone him tomorrow.

Tomorrow's the middle of the week already, and I'm going to the English Department meeting rather than teaching my 3 PM class. Thank goodness this idiocy will be over soon. I long to read good books instead of banal student paragraphs.

This morning I woke up late after a delicious ten-hour sleep. I took $100 out of my Anchor account and went to the Dime in Kings Plaza, where I paid off my loan. It was getting late and I didn't want to wait around for my bankbook, so they're mailing it to me.

I paid $10 for my gas this morning; I'll have to watch how much I drive now that I'm not using Dad's credit card.

Last night it got down to 30° and we had steam heat for the first time since April. The trees are almost bare by this time, and I've been wearing my winter jacket.

Fifteen years ago this week President Kennedy was assassinated. To my students, JFK is as distant as FDR was to me – just a figure on the front of a coin.

Tuesday, November 21, 1978

8 PM. Yesterday I wrote, rather stupidly, "I hate the fact that I have to teach such scum as Rosa Cordero. " Today I found this note in my mailbox at school:

"Para mi querido amor: Yo quisiero escribe estas lineas para decirle lo mucho que te a o, quiero decirle los momentos amoroso y apasionados que yo pas contingo en mis sueños. . ."

Even I could figure that out. On the bottom of the ripped-out loose-leaf paper, there was a red lipstick outline of a woman's lips with the words *"¡Este beso es para te, amor mio!"* And it was signed *"Te enamorada, Anonima."*

"My love, Anonymous"? Good Lord, what have I gotten myself into? The letter was phony-poetic Spanish; John translated the whole thing for me:

". . . I love you like a desperate one. . . I hope these words do not offend you, but I must say them because I cannot contain my soul. For my love for you is the most beautiful and veritable love that I have felt all my life and it doesn't pain me to confess this. . . Now I despair with great sadness because I think this great love is not requited. . ."

Just before I had gone up to my mailbox, Rosa asked me if I had checked my mail yesterday. I said I did, but very early in the day, and she said a girl gave her a note to put in my mailbox.

I gave John an essay she handed in yesterday and asked him if the handwriting is similar. "I don't have to look at the handwriting," John said. "Read the essay."

And I read: ". . . I have at KCC a crush on a very special teacher named that I will not emention [sic]. He know who he is. I won't tell him my feelings. The way I feel above [sic] him."

I am flabbergasted by this. No one's ever fallen in love with me like this. And look who it is: a moronic slob, probably a psychotic. I don't feel at all flattered;

it makes me queasy, as if she's intruded into my personal life.

I've been asking colleagues, friends and family how to deal with this, and everyone says I should ignore it, so that's probably the best bet. Until Rosa comes to me and confesses her "love," I don't have to say anything.

I had thought she was over her crush on me. But even Rosa seems to understand that I couldn't possibly reciprocate; I hope she knows, deep down, that this is just an infatuation.

What does intrigue me (and undoubtedly there's first-rate fictional material in this) is why Rosa chose *me* to idealize. Was it just that I was polite to her, as few other people are? I'm hardly a romantic figure.

Maybe this will help me understand my own crushes better – not that I take them seriously, anyway.

This morning I got a haircut, and then Wesley and I straightened out the half-titles; we've decided to go for vague ones like "Objects," "Artifacts," "Families." Bobs thought using titles as half-titles would be confusing.

So now the book moves into the production stage, going to the designer. Six months from now the book will be a living thing; you can't help comparing it to a baby.

Today I got a book from the brilliant Opal L. Nations, and a book and a card from Susan Schaeffer's friend Linda Lerner, as well as several rejections, an acceptance of a very traditional story ("A Distant Death") by a very traditional magazine, *The University of Portland Review*; and a letter from the English chair of the University of New Orleans telling me to submit my recommendations very soon.

I have no recommendations, really; I've always been embarrassed by asking for them, but now I suppose I'll have to. Of course I'm not sure I want to move to New Orleans; I definitely don't want to go there in the spring. Am I such a coward that I would jeopardize my academic career because of neurotic fears?

Wednesday, November 22, 1978

10 PM. I feel tired and very glad I don't have to work tomorrow. This is my first four-day weekend since Rosh Hashona, and I've looked forward to it for quite some time.

My shoulder has been aching. I wonder if I'm old enough to get bursitis. Enough kvetching, though. I have been sleeping fitfully this week, and my wisdom tooth has stopped aching.

This morning I got a call from Donald Stauffer, Director of Graduate study at SUNY/Albany. He thought he might be able to get me a fellowship for spring, and I said he should go ahead and try.

But later, I sent him a letter advising him I'd prefer a fellowship for the fall. I don't really want to go to Albany in January. Part of it, of course, is the neurotic fear I wrote about yesterday. But I want – and I know this will sound absurd – "to finish out my ten years."

Since the summer of 1969, when I began keeping a diary, when I began college, when I ended a long year of isolation, I've felt that my life really began that year. Next August I will have completed ten years of these diaries, and after that, I feel, I will be ready for the next step in life.

Even though I am still in this room, I have left it enough so that I am a part of the world. If I can finish my ten years of these diaries, I'll somehow feel complete; I'll be ready to die, even.

Michael Metcalf, a counselor at Kingsborough, was killed in a car crash Friday night. Sheila had mentioned it Saturday night; a friend of hers, another counselor, was very upset. I had seen Michael in the elevator all this term, but not until today, when I saw his black-bordered photo in *The Scepter*, did I realize why I always felt I'd known him from somewhere else.

He was a delegate to the University Student Senate from Hunter when I represented Richmond. He was a very competent, very well-liked guy, and no, I can't believe that I saw him on his last day alive.

Life is incredibly fragile – the murders and suicides by that cult in Guyana amazed everyone, I think, because these people were alive and well one minute and dead the next.

Classes went well today. Now that the term is ending and I'll probably be laid off (*The Scepter* said "adjunct faculty will be hardest hit by the budget cuts"), I feel at home at Kingsborough. I've got friends on the faculty, among the staff, and I've even gotten attached to some of my students.

Speaking of students, Rosa came to me after class and asked if I got the note. "I haven't checked my mailbox," I said, unable to think of anything else. "I'm in a hurry now, so I can't talk."

"I just wrote, like, my feelings for you, and I hope you don't become mad."

"I won't get mad," I said, rushing to the elevator. But that was not dealing with it.

This evening I went over to Ronna's and watched her knead dough for some pastries she was making for tomorrow's dinner at her aunt's. Billy and Robby were acting like wild creatures, as usual, and snickering about "dick" being short for "detective."

It was good just hanging out. Billy called me "a friend of the family," and I like that. Six years ago, the night before Thanksgiving, Wednesday, November 22, 1972, Ronna and I had our first date.

I remember that night clearly. I can see Ronna in her blue turtleneck, sniffling into a paper towel (there were no tissues in the bathroom) in the right-hand side of the Midwood Theater audience.

We saw Rohmer's *Chloe in the Afternoon*, had tea and muffins at The Foursome, and sat on the floor of my room until 2 AM. When I kissed her goodnight, she said, "I hope you don't catch my cold." I didn't.

<u>Thursday, November 23, 1978</u>

7 PM. Today was one of the most depressing Thanksgivings I can remember. I've never really enjoyed Thanksgiving and don't see why Mom has to make a big production over dinner.

She's been in severe pain since last night; evidently she has a severe toothache. I feel sorry for her, but I also can't help feeling angry with her for making today such a down day.

The weather didn't help; it's dark and raw and rainy. All in all, not the kind of day you feel like giving thanks. I know I have much to be thankful for, but I didn't want to do it today.

I slept poorly last night, annoyed with myself for thinking about school while I'm on vacation. I kept coming back to Rosa and her "love" for me, to my other students' problems: Ivy Siegel with her Harvard boyfriend, unhappy in a community college; Maria Martinez, who wants me to give her extra work so she "can become a good writer"; John Petrowski, who seems retarded and is the butt of the class's jokes.

Yesterday some professor asked me how I liked my term at Kingsborough; I told him I was enjoying it. I didn't want it to become a real part of my life, but it did. I thought I could just teach there eight hours a week and collect my salary, but involuntarily, I've become involved with the school and the people there.

And the emptiness of today makes me wonder whether this is how I'll feel when the term ends. At 27 (and about six months), I still don't know what I'm doing with my life and that bothers me terribly.

I have no direction except in my writing, and even that seems gone now. I feel old, in a bad way – as if my body were aging every day. Yet yesterday I got enraged when the old lady at the Kings Plaza newsstand said, "*Sonny*, don't read the magazines here."

I answered another ad from a guy in the *Voice* last night – at 4 AM, when I couldn't sleep. I've decided I want to be Ronna's friend and not her lover. I'm just not that attracted to her anymore, and I have to make that clear to her soon. I love her more than I love any other friend, though, and I don't want to lose her.

I feel a bit – no, a great deal – of dissatisfaction with my life. Or maybe this is just a bad mood. A dozen years ago on the Friday after Thanksgiving, I consulted a psychiatrist for the first time. It was scary, being in Dr. Lippman's dark, African-themed office, but I felt I had nowhere else to go.

I was a mess then, and now I'm an older, more intelligent, less neurotic, somewhat successful mess. I have a bad headache that I woke up with. I feel fat. I can't believe spring will really come, and I hate writing sentences like these.

When I get these depressions, I'm impossible. Let me write about other people: Teresa got a job in the public relations division of the New York public library. She start Monday, but she's not excited about it because the pay is so low (the benefits, however – as in any city job – are very good). But it does sound very interesting. Gary and Betty went to his parents for dinner, so they're getting along better now.

Grandpa Herb told us Uncle Jack's now in the nursing home next to Peninsula Hospital. Jack doesn't know much of what's going on. Aunt Sydelle is seeing a man who takes her out only on Fridays and Sundays, and Mom and Dad suspect he's married.

In the *Authors Guild Bulletin*, I read that Teresa's ex Fletcher Newton has become president of Cambridge Books, owned by the New York Times. Alice did not go to Boulder for the holidays after all; she had dinner today with Philip.

I've been reading Richard Reeves' *Convention*, about the Democrats in New York in 1976. I miss politics and being a politician. Then again, I guess I *am* one.

Friday, November 24, 1978

6 PM. I awoke to the sounds of vomiting this morning. Mom was in such pain from her tooth that Dad went to Larry Rothenberg's and got some Codeine and Demerol, and I guess Mom couldn't

tolerate it, because she was retching and throwing up violently.

Dad managed to get her downtown to the endodontist in the Williamsburgh Savings Bank Building. Mom vomited again in the doctor's office, but he fixed her cap. There was an abscess, the nerve had died, and there was nowhere for the pus to go. It's draining now, and Mom's still in pain and is running a fever; she's in bed.

Jonny has the same horror of vomiting that I once did and ran down to the basement this morning. He later explained to me that he vomited the night his friend's father was killed, and since then he's associated vomiting with death. I understood but didn't know what I could do to help.

Marc took my car to Flushing, so I got to Manhattan for my lunch date with Alice by bus and subway. I had expected to eat out, but Alice prepared a Brooklyn-style lunch of bagels, tuna, cheese and salad.

On her kitchen table was her "Thought for the Day: Fun builds character – P. Breglio." It replaced "Work builds character – A. Trifonikis." (Andreas is working in Miami now.)

Alice told me she's been discouraged with the BMI musical comedy workshop; this week, when she and her partner performed three songs, Lehman Engel tore them apart. He's a martinet and dislikes Alice's work; in fact, he ignores all the women (he's gay and takes out the men from the class).

Alice got a letter from the BC journalism program asking her about her recent working experiences and inviting comments on how relevant her coursework was. Alice replied that her BC classes were no help and mentioned that Prof. Miller advised Alice she'd never make it as a writer.

Alice is still looking for a job. Richard got her an interview at Rogers & Cowan, and they'd hire her in a minute, at $20,000 a year, but Alice doesn't want to do PR work and plan ad campaigns for perfume. When Alice complained recently about money, her brother reminded her that their father never made more than $10,000 a year in his life.

Alice generously gave me review copies of several books and we walked down Eighth Street, getting the subway uptown. We were hoping to see *Movie, Movie* at the Sutton, but we arrived too late, as there was an incredible line.

Coming out of the last show were Mason and Stacy, and we started talking and decided to go with them to La Crêpe. I hadn't talked to Stacy in years (or should I say the reverse?) but she told me she was looking forward to my book, which Mason had told her about.

Evidently Stacy's parents split up; she's dividing her time between Brooklyn and Rockaway, trying to get into grad school in arts management, and still hoping for a musical career. One of the first things she asked me was if it was true that Ivan was married; when I told her he was, she was pumping me for information which I didn't have. Interesting.

Apparently Stacy's still friends with Mona; Alice mentioned that one of her friends at *Seventeen* was on the jury in a case where Mona argued brilliantly and won. (I'd heard Mona was doing well from Ronna via Leroy and from Teresa via Costas.) We mentioned Scott and the Wexlers and Avis, and Stacy suggested that I have a party inviting everyone from BC.

It was a pleasant lunch. For one thing, I was glad to see Mason, and I rode back to Brooklyn with him and Stacy and he gave me a lift home from Kings Highway. Stacy looks well and I understand what attracted me to her years ago – and what turned me off.

Saturday, November 25, 1978

6 PM. My diary entries lately have been pretty stale.
This is due to a combination of factors. Wesley's
editing, though very shrewd, has made more careful
in my writing; so has teaching grammar exclusively.
I've been hyper-aware of the flaws in my style and
have been over-editing in my mind. My writing has
become more controlled, more carefully correct – but
I've lost vitality.

This is one reason I have written hardly any fiction.
Now that I'm a "real" writer, I've gotten a fear of
committing myself on paper; I've stopped
experimenting, trying out weird things and allowing
myself the possibility of flopping on my face.

But – I recognize (I reckon) The Problem now; or
mebbe it'll clear up (no, verbal cute-isms ain't gonna
do the trick, pardner. Jes' don't *work* so gol-darned
hard).

This is apropos of my purchase of my 1979 diary at
Barchas Book Store this afternoon. You Grayson
diary fans from way back when will recall that the 18-
year-old Richie bought his 1969 diary (same National
Time-Line, #55-148) at a half-price sale at Barchas.

On the way home, my car hit 60,000 miles. I was
stopped at Kings Highway and Avenue J, by that
yeshiva which was a private school Jonny attended

for a few days during the '68 teachers' strike. I looked down and the odometer said 60000.9 – another tenth of a mile and I would have missed it. So, as Eric Sevareid might say (I always thought his shoulders were too big for my TV screen), "it's been a day of milestones." Or millstones.

My airline ticket arrived from Delta right on the day it turned frigid and I needed gloves for the first time this season. I'm terrified of flying, but I'm going to do it; I need the warmth of Florida and the sight of my grandparents too much. I'll take along one of those anti-phobia books I read this summer. (Was there a summer?)

Nice Thing From the Week: Riding up Flatlands Avenue to Ronna's, an old LIU student, Stuart Charney, honked next to me. I may not like teaching, but I do like having taught. (Secretly I've wanted to be Mr. Chips all along.)

Last night I moseyed over to Ronna's, where she gave me a career update: she doesn't want to work on a weekly, only a daily. I have no way of knowing if her goal is realistic. I advised her to read *Editor & Publisher* and everything about journalism she can get her hands on. I want to spur Ronna on the way Andreas does for Alice.

We drove out to Kennedy Airport, and that sort of opened up the evening: it was a clear, cold night.

Back at Ronna's house, we had tea and watched TV while Susan called to tell Ronna how crazy Marvin's getting because he hasn't heard how he did on the bar exams. (I bet he failed.) Susan, Ronna said, was annoyed to find me over again and purposely talked longer.

That being the case and for the all-around mental health of Ronna, I told her I'd bow out of next Saturday's dinner. I'd really like to go but I don't eat shrimp (she's cooking tempura) and am not sure I'm up for an evening with Susan, Marvin and John. (I'm sure Alison, Brad and Andrew would be less offensive.) Ronna wouldn't have time for me and would get mad if I acted aloof or annoyed, the way I did at Susan's.

I hugged and kissed Ronna in a cuddly, sweater-y, winter sort of way. It ain't passion, but it's tender. (Yes, I admit I'm *still* very attracted to Stacy. I told Ronna about Stacy's questioning me about Ivan. "Another broken heart," she said.)

George sent a wonderful letter, about his grandfather, the Colonel, and bike-riding and nominating me for the CCLM grants committee. I got five rejections today and an acceptance from *Snapdragon*.

Sunday, November 26, 1978

4 PM on the first really cold day of the winter. It didn't get out of 20°s last night, and since I have no steam in my room, I had to make do with an extra blanket. Today's high was a blustery 35° and some snow is expected tomorrow morning, although it will probably change to rain later in the day.

I've just come back from Long Island. David Gross called me this morning, saying he was at his brother's fiancée's parents' house in Oyster Bay. David said he wanted to move to New York and "get established as a writer." He told me I could introduce him to all my "friends in the publishing world."

I drove out to meet David and his brother Jeff for lunch at the Howard Johnson's in East Norwich, on Northern Boulevard. I hadn't taken a long drive in many months, and it was a pleasure.

David looked the same, though his brother lost so much weight, I didn't recognize him. I gently disabused David of the noting of coming to Manhattan and "the literary world."

When he told me I could introduce him to "the New York little magazine people," I tried not to laugh and explained that I don't know anyone, that little magazines are widely scattered all over the country, and that he has as much chance getting accepted from Maine as from Manhattan.

He quit his job in Bath as head of his father's plant and was willing to spend $500 a month for an apartment – "but not in the Village with the faggots." ("Gay people," I coolly corrected him – and felt glad I did.)

I told David he can write stories from anywhere, that living in New York was fine, but that launching a literary career was not a good reason for moving, that I'd just gotten acceptances from magazines in Oregon and Montana.

I was aided in this by Jeff, who detests New York and its people. They've been very wealthy all their lives and so can afford to play with the idea of being artists. I felt rather proud about my struggles with money, my living at home ("in the slums of Flatbush," I almost said.)

Playing "poor kid" is a new favorite game of mine. I make vulgar remarks about other people's money (i.e., "Wow, you must really be rich. Is your father a millionaire?") and point out my own noble, artistic poverty.

Last night I worked on some concrete poems based on pristine terms like "windows," "justification" and "rivers." This morning I came up with a one-page

"New Testament Diet" ("How did Jesus shed those unsightly pounds and become the slim Savior we know him as today?") which would be great as part of a stand-up comedy routine, though I don't know if I can find a publisher for it. Maybe I should become a comedian and forget about writing literary stuff.

Anyway, I do feel creative today, and energetic; maybe yesterday's realization that I've been too serious about my writing has liberated me. After all, I wouldn't have written "Hitler," "Real People" or "Chief Justice Burger" for a book – *too undignified* – yet that was what's going in the book. Why? *Because* it's weird and Richard Grayson-ish. That's what got me where I am today, with *Disjointed Fictions* next to Graves' *I, Claudius* on the shelf at the Eighth Street Bookshop.

This isn't my usual glum winter Sunday. Two more full weeks of teaching, two days, the final exams and final grades – and I'm free to get depressed as often as I choose.

Monday, November 27, 1978

7 PM. Throughout this past week, we've been seeing images of incredible violence on TV. First there was the murder of Congressman Ryan and the reporter at

the airstrip in Guyana by the followers of the Rev. Jim Jones.

Next there were those horrible photos of 900 decomposing bodies of People's Temple members – the mess recalled Masada, the piling up of corpses reminded me of the Holocaust.

Today San Francisco Mayor George Moscone was shot by a city official he'd recently fired; then the man ran across City Hill to the Board of Supervisors meeting and shot gay activist supervisor Harvey Milk.

Immediately I recalled (and of course the networks replayed) the scenes of Mayor Moscone a week ago regretting his one-time appointment of Jim Jones as Housing Chairman and of Milk breaking down in tears at the funeral of his friend Leo Ryan. He had no idea (oh, this sounds banal) he too would be dead in a week.

They say the shooting had no connection with the Guyana massacre, but I believe violence conditions us to expect and even to perpetrate further violence. Human life is so terribly fragile as it is, and here people make it their business to destroy others' lives on their own.

I don't know what to make of it. Not for ten years have I felt the world to be such a dangerous place, not

since the assassinations of Martin Luther King, Jr. and
Robert Kennedy and the Chicago convention riot of
1968.

Today was a hostile day, anyway – there was snow
most of the day. I can't remember snow in November
before. A bad sign of a long winter or is it a false
start? Driving to Kingsborough was treacherous, as I
slid all over the rad.

Only a few students showed up for my 12:40 class.
Rosa handed me a so-called term paper that was
actually a word-for-word copy of an article by
Jonathan Kozol. I have to give her an F on it, but I
worry: she is capable of great violence, I'm certain,
and she's crazy.

If she can love so passionately, couldn't she also try to
kill me? I know this is my imagination running wild,
but an F isn't much different than being fired from a
$10,000 job with the city of San Francisco.

Rosa has so much emotional energy invested in me,
or rather, in her image of me. Last year a teacher was
shot by dead by a student he failed. If anyone is
capable of murdering me, Rosa is. I know I have to
pass her in the course. Jesus, I feel as though I'm
living in an Alfred Hitchcock movie, and it doesn't
feel very good.

For the first time in my life I got stuck on an elevator today. I went into the elevator, pushed the button for the third floor (where the English Department is) and noting happened. I was alone. I rang the alarm; I called out. Finally I pressed the "Door Open" button and the door opened to the first floor; I had been there all the time.

The snow turned to freezing rain by the time I made my way to the 3 PM class. Some of the accumulation melted, and driving home was a bit easier. It's raining now, as temperatures are rising. It's so weird to see snow on the streets again; it's as if winter had always been here, as if there never was a summer.

Last night Mom and Dad went to a wedding of one of Dad's cousin's sons. Aunt Sydelle was there with her boyfriend, who's given her a magnificent ring – not an engagement ring, but it is filled with diamonds. Dad's Uncle Benny, the groom's grandfather, danced like a youngster even though he has a pacemaker and is 83. Uncle Joe was the only other brother there, as Grandma Sylvia, Uncle Daniel and Uncle Bernard are all in Florida.

The Authors Guild sent me their model contract; I don't have much protection in my contract, but I felt I couldn't negotiate.

Tuesday, November 28, 1978

7 PM. A peculiar day. I dreamed dozens of dreams
last night and did not want to get up this morning. So
when my car died on Ralph and Avenue N on my
way home from the bank, I took that as an omen that
fate didn't want me to go to school. I could have
made it on time: the AAA boosted me at about noon,
the usual time I leave, but I didn't want to go in.

I called Evalin, but she was out sick too, so I gave my
name to the student aide. I can't help feeling a bit
guilty, as I used to do when I stayed out of high
school because I was avoiding something. I dread
going back tomorrow; I'm just sick of teaching and
sick of Kingsborough.

Two weeks from tonight I'll be free – sixteen more
classes – ten more days. Yet I can see where I'll be
depressed staying home and *not* working. The winter
is so deadly and I almost always get depressed; that's
why I'm so glad Avis is coming and that I'm going to
Florida after she leaves. If I know nothing else about
my mental health, I know that inactivity makes me
very depressed. So it's a heads-I-lose, tails-you-win
kind of thing.

Books help. In the past 24 hours I've been reading
Carolyn Heilbrun's *Toward a Recognition of Androgyny*;
Dennis Cooper's *Little Caesar* magazine (he sent it to

me for free); various popular periodical; and J.L.
Dillard's *All-American English*.

I went to the CCLM office and used their library; also
I got their list of fall grants, but I don't have the urge
to submit everywhere as I used to. For one thing, I
don't have that much unpublished, unaccepted work;
for another, getting published in little magazines
doesn't matter as much as it used to.

And the cost of submitting is so expensive. The
Consumer Price Index reached 200 today, meaning
that *everything* costs twice as much as it did in 1967.

When I was a high school senior, gasoline went for
30¢ a gallon, postage stamps cost a nickel, buses and
subways were 20¢, and rarely did a paperback book
cost more than $1.25. I guess we paid a couple of
dollars to get into a movie. I remember pizza at 20¢ a
slice.

Dad used to tell me about the low prices during the
Depression, and I seem to have the same stories now.
Dad is probably making the same salary he made in
1967 – but that means his real income has been
halved. Hell, even in 1972, Dad gave me $40 a week
allowance and never missed it.

I applied for various jobs in the Sunday *Times*,
including a position as editorial assistant to Eliot
Janeway, the economist. I'm just not certain what it is

I want to do. I know I want time to read and write, but more than that, I just don't know. I am tired of teaching, that's for sure.

Grandpa Herb and Grandma Ethel stopped by on their way home from NYU Hospital. The doctors found no spread of the rash but warned Grandma Ethel that she has cancer and must return every six weeks for three years. They laughed themselves silly when they heard of Grandma Ethel's health-food diet.

Isaac Bashevis Singer was interviewed in the Sunday *Times Magazine,* and I was relieved to learn that he wrote nothing for ten years; that gives me some hope. A great deal is made of the "sufferings" of writers (I've read a couple of essays on Lowell and Sexton recently). I don't think writers "suffer" more than other people. Perhaps their suffering is more interesting, that's all.

Wednesday, November 29, 1978

8 PM. The National Weather Bureau's forecast is for a mild winter this year. Let's hope so. Most of the snow has melted by now. I feel free, knowing that I have only one class each of the next two days – and on Friday I'm having my students write, so I don't have to prepare anything.

Less than two weeks to go and you can feel it around school. Everyone's looking ahead to finals and Christmas vacation. I had two pretty good classes today; I suppose I do have good rapport with my students even if I dislike teaching.

I gave Rosa back her term paper, which she vehemently denied copying. I asked her the meaning of some of the words in her essay, and she grew exasperated: "I don't know, I just *wrote* it!"

Her tutor sent me a note that she missed two consecutive sessions and is being dropped from tutoring. In between classes, I had my own tutoring session with Maria Martinez, a lovely Cuban girl who wants extra help – and I gave her tips on style. Now if *Maria* were in love with me. . . But of course she's too intelligent for that. ("I've noticed you often put yourself down," Maria told me. "You shouldn't do that.") Anyway, I suppose I have a grudging affection for most of my students.

This week's mail has brought nothing but rejections and junk mail. After last week, I was expecting an acceptance a day. David Gross sent me a story to criticize and help him get published; he's living in his family in Newton Centre now.

This morning I got up early and went to the post office and to do some shopping. At Christie's I met my friend John, one of the interns, who lives a few blocks away. Mikey called and asked if I could participate in a mock *voir dire* at his law school tonight, but I wouldn't have been able to make it in time. (Too bad – I might have enjoyed it.)

Last night I kept notes on my dreams. I wake up after most dreams – generally every 90 minutes. What I've discovered is that there is no dream-remembering mechanism in my brain; if I don't write my dreams down, most evaporate without a trace by morning – even the ones I'm certain I will remember.

Dreams are very boring, so I won't copy all my notes here. In one dream, I was in a supermarket and met Dad's cousin Ike and his father-in-law, Uncle Nathan (who died years ago).

Then I went to Grandpa Nat's house and saw Grandpa Nat, Grandma Sylvia and Aunt Sydelle (I told Sydelle that Dad said she looked good at the wedding – which he did, just yesterday).

As I left, Grandpa Nat pressed twenty dollars into my hand. I didn't realize it until I was walking away. I ran back, hoping to return the money, but he ran upstairs so quickly I couldn't catch him.

Remembering that he was in a nursing home, I wondered how he could run so fast. "I love you!" I shouted upstairs to Grandpa Nat, but he couldn't come down.

That dream symbolizes my inability to reach Grandpa Nat any longer. I can't communicate with him rationally; I can't make him understand my feelings toward him. Every once in a while, I find myself remembering that he's brain-damaged, and I stop short: *How can it be?*

In another dream, I was staying with a young couple who were living with an older married couple with two grown sons. The old husband was having an affair with the young girl, an affair to which both spouses consented.

The family of four wanted to be alone together ("family time"), so I left one room only to enter another to find my friends having an intimate discussion ("It's couple time, sorry.") I felt alone until a little kitten jumped on my lap to comfort me. *You* figure that out.

Thursday, November 30, 1978

1 PM. This morning I wrote my first story in nearly three months. It feels good to finally get something good down on paper. Even as I put the first sheaf in the typewriter, I felt very clumsy and nervous; I made three typos in my name and address.

But after seven pages, I finished what I think is a publishable story, "Relentless Days, Corduroy Nights." I used the same expanding sentence device I employed in "Roman Buildings" and "Appearance House." It makes for a dreamlike story.

The ending was dream I had last night. Ronna and I were on a terrace, watching boats pass by below. A Hispanic family on a boat overturned and a little boy drowned. We looked down on them and I cried, "Oh, Ronna, life is so relentless. So much happens. How can we keep up with it all? There's no time for anything."

I'm sure I couldn't have written the story on any other day but Thursday when I don't have the pressure of leaving the house at noon. This makes me certain that with less outside pressure, I *will* be able to write as I used to.

It's such a relief; for a while I thought I was never going to write another story again. I got a letter from Gretchen Johnsen of *Gargoyle*. She and Rick Peabody want to use "What About Us Grils?" in place of "Minimum Competency Test" in their double fiction issue. I agreed that it's a stronger piece and gave them my okay.

George Jochnowitz wrote that he enjoyed the stories I sent him. (He caught an inconsistency in one of them.) And Michael Lally sent me a wonderful letter.

I could fall in love with him, I know it. I admire him so much and he said he loved "Go Not to Lethe," which I'd sent him. Michael said to keep in touch and so I sent him a copy of *Disjointed Fictions*.

I had another dream last night; in it, I was greedily eating peanuts and raisins. When I awoke, my pillow was covered with saliva; I had been drooling all over the place. Last night I relaxed by watching *Billy Jack*, a simplistic but well-intentioned movie.

In a couple of hours I'm teaching comparison and contrast, but I'm not too prepared. Hell, it's the end of the term and I'm sick of the whole thing, as are my students.

I spoke to Ronna last night; she and Alison had dinner at Shakespeare's in the Village. Last weekend Phil came in and they had a nice time. She hasn't yet heard from any of the newspaper editors she wrote to. Next week she's got an interview with the Placement Service at Penn State.

Tomorrow Ronna and I have that cystic fibrosis disco party at Studio 54; I'm kind of sorry I bothered with it now (as I knew I would be).

My car didn't start this morning, so we had to call the AAA again; I'm afraid the Comet needs a new battery.

I haven't heard from Avis in weeks; I hope everything is all right and that she's still coming in as planned.

It's a sunny day, but I haven't been out yet. I cut myself twice while shaving and in squeezing a pimple. I made a red blotch (*kinnahora*, my skin has been very clear lately, but now, with winter and steam, my pores tend to close up).

Tomorrow's December. It's unbelievable that 1978 should have gone so fast. What I said in my dream – and in my story – is trite and banal, but it's so true. It pains me how little I've done, how much I've yet to do. If I do have a real enemy, it's my Timex ticking away.

www.ingramcontent.com/pod-product-compliance
Lightning Source LLC
Chambersburg PA
CBHW020848090426
42736CB00008B/292